SHACKLETON

THE BOSS

About the author

Michael Smith gave up his career as a leading business and
political journalist to write the best-selling biography,
An Unsung Hero – Tom Crean, Antarctic Explorer.
He has a life-long interest in Polar exploration and has also written
I Am Just Going Outside – Captain Oates, Antarctic Tragedy and
Tom Crean: Ice Man, The Adventures of an Irish Antarctic Hero,
an account specially written for children.
*Shackleton: The Boss, The Remarkable Adventures of a
Heroic Antarctic Explorer*
is Michael's second book for children.

About the Illustrator

Annie Brady is a student at The National College of Art and Design,
Dublin and works as a freelance illustrator.

SHACKLETON THE BOSS

The Remarkable Adventures of a Heroic Antarctic Explorer

Michael Smith

Illustrations by Annie Brady

The Collins Press

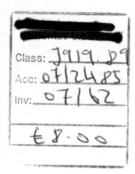
First published in 2004 by
The Collins Press,
West Link Park,
Doughcloyne,
Wilton,
Cork

This edition 2006

British Library Cataloguing in Publication data.

ISBN-10: 1-905172-27-3
ISBN-13: 978-1905172-27-6

Printed in Ireland by ColourBooks Ltd.
Design by Artmark

CONTENTS

INTRODUCTION

Explorers are special. The strong human urge to stand on ground where no one has stood before, or sail across oceans where no ships have sailed, has produced many of history's greatest heroes.

The famous names – Alexander the Great, Marco Polo, Christopher Columbus, Ferdinand Magellan, Captain James Cook, David Livingstone and Neil Armstrong – ring down through the ages.

The early explorers overcame great challenges and constant danger to uncover the secrets of the earth's unknown lands and seas. But of these exploits the most outstanding tales of adventure and hardship are set at the very bottom of the world – the frozen wastes of Antarctica, the last continent to be explored.

And the most remarkable tale of all is the story of the celebrated explorer, Sir Ernest Shackleton.

Though Ernest Shackleton was born among the green pastures of Ireland, his name will always be associated with the ice-covered wilderness of the Antarctic. He made four epic voyages to the ice and snow during a short life and left a lasting mark on history.

His amazing exploits and survival against impossible odds are the stuff of legend. Someone once said that Shackleton lived life 'like a mighty rushing wind'.

Shackleton was a great leader who always put the safety of his men first. He took men to the wildest and most dangerous place on earth, but always brought them back safely. He inspired men to achieve great deeds.

Those who knew Sir Ernest Shackleton called him the Boss.

Chapter 1

DREAMING OF ADVENTURE

As a child Ernest Shackleton longed for far away places. He dreamt of travelling to the remote parts of the earth and exploring the unknown. He wanted to go where no one had been before.

At night he read books and comics which filled his head with the exploits of great voyages to distant lands. A favourite tale was *20,000 Leagues Under the Sea*, the classic book by Jules Verne about the submarine, *Nautilus*, that roamed the oceans under the mysterious Captain Nemo.

A fallen tree trunk in his garden became a ship's cabin and each day he sailed the seven seas in search of adventure.

Once he took a shovel into his back garden in Ireland and began digging a hole all the way to Australia. He did not get very far.

The parts of the world which held a special appeal for Ernest Shackleton were the North and South Poles where there is only ice and snow. He read all the books he could find about them. No one had ever been to either.

Ernest Shackleton's dream was to be the first man to leave his footprints in the two most remote places on earth. What he could

never have expected was that his true-life adventures would be far greater, and more amazing, than anything in his dreams.

The Shackleton family ran a modest farm among the rich, green pastures of County Kildare, Ireland. Ernest was born in a large house at Kilkea, near Athy, in 1874. He was one of ten children – eight girls and two boys – who enjoyed a happy childhood, playing in the nearby fields.

When he was ten years old, his family abandoned the peaceful farm in Ireland and moved across the Irish Sea to the busy city of London. It was a big change. Ernest Shackleton did well at sports like boxing and football but found the new school hard going.

Ernest's father, who had sold the farm to become a doctor, wanted his son to follow in his footsteps and treat the sick. But Ernest dreamed of running away to sea.

Once, he took some friends to see a ship moored at London Bridge on the River Thames. The boys tried to enlist as sailors on the ship. The ship's chief steward took one look at the young lads and promptly threw them out. Ernest never forgot being turned away from the ship. He vowed it would never happen again.

Shortly after his sixteenth birthday, Ernest Shackleton broke the news to his father that he did not want to become a doctor and begged to be allowed to leave school and join the navy instead. His father was very disappointed, but did not stand in the youngster's way.

Chapter 2

JOURNEY TO THE ICE

The first ship Ernest Shackleton worked on was called the *Hoghton Tower*, a cargo vessel bound for Chile in South America. He was enrolled at the lowest level, as ship's boy. His wage was the tiny sum of one shilling (5p) a month – which is worth less than 4 euro a month today.

Life on board was harsh. Work was hard and when duties were finished, the sailors were cramped together below decks.

To reach Chile, the ship had to sail around the stormy Cape Horn at the very tip of South America. It is one of the roughest sea passages in the world and the ship was tossed around so violently that some crewmen were injured.

But Ernest was in his element. He loved the sea. He had found the adventurous life he wanted. Soon after returning home from his first voyage, Ernest Shackleton set sail once again.

He spent the next ten years sailing round the world, learning about the sea and ships. It was a good life. But he realised it was not enough to satisfy his thirst for adventure.

In 1900 Shackleton read that an expedition was being put together to explore the unknown continent of Antarctica.

It was a chance to fulfil another of his dreams – a journey to the ice and snow. Luckily Shackleton knew a man whose father helped pay for the expedition. It was just the break he needed and Shackleton was accepted for the voyage. It was a dream come true and it was also a big step into the unknown.

Few men had ever set foot on the Antarctic Continent, the coldest and most hostile place on earth. There were no reliable maps and no native people to teach explorers how to survive the freezing conditions.

No one knew what to expect when the expedition reached the frozen continent. Or whether they would ever return.

The weather in the Antarctic is brutal. Temperatures often fall below -40° Celsius (-40° Fahrenheit) and even in the slightly warmer summer months it can be -20°C (-4°F). The lowest temperature ever recorded was taken in Antarctica – an unbelievable -89.6°C (-129°F). At home today a typical freezer is only set at -20°C (-4°F).

The Antarctic expedition sailed from London in the summer of 1901. By chance, the expedition ship sailed from near the spot where Shackleton had been turned down on his first attempt to go to sea many years before.

The expedition ship, which was specially strengthened to withstand the crushing pressure of the ice, was built in Scotland and named *Discovery*. And the captain was Robert Scott.

Discovery crossed the oceans and headed for New Zealand, the last place they would stop to take on fresh supplies before plunging into the unknown. Next stop would be the icy wilderness of the Antarctic.

Nothing grows in the Antarctic so every scrap of food would have to be carried on sledges. It meant that *Discovery* was weighed down with supplies and food to feed the men for two or three years of exploration. Also on deck were sheep to provide fresh meat, and 23 howling dogs. The dogs would later help the men drag their sledges once they arrived on land.

The only wildlife, such as penguins and seals, were to be found on the shoreline. Consequently, once they left the shore and moved inland, the men would have to pull their food and equipment on sledges.

As *Discovery* pulled away from the dock and headed towards the ice, one of Scott's sailors climbed the rigging to get a better look at the cheering crowds. But the sailor lost his footing and crashed to the deck below. He was killed instantly. This was a grim reminder of the dangers the expedition faced.

Weeks later Shackleton caught his first sight of the great white continent. It was an awesome place of untamed natural beauty.

Not long after, Shackleton had a lucky escape of his own. He and the other explorers wanted to get a better view of the frozen land which lay sprawled in front of them. The plan was to send a man hundreds of metres into the sky in a hot air balloon so he could see what the local terrain was like.

Captain Scott had made the first ascent, gaining a marvellous view

of Antarctica before him. Next up was Shackleton, eager to scan the horizon and to snatch a photograph of the unknown territory where the explorers were planning to go.

Suddenly, the balloon shot up to a dizzy height of around 250m (825ft) – much too high! Swaying in the strong wind, Shackleton grasped the side of the balloon's basket. He could see a flat plain of ice and snow, a scene of endless whiteness.

No one had ever seen this far into the interior of the Antarctic and Shackleton quickly took a photograph, the first picture of the route to the Pole.

It might have been his last photo. When the balloon came back to ground it was checked for faults. To Shackleton's horror, it was discovered that the balloon was highly dangerous. Only luck had stopped the balloon plunging to the ground like a stone.

Danger is never far away in the Antarctic. On one occasion, a man was walking along the top of a hill near the water's edge when he slipped on the ice and plunged down a slippery slope into the freezing water. He was never seen again.

Another explorer suffered severe frostbite on his foot when temperatures dropped sharply during a sledging trip. His shipmates knew that unless the frozen limb could be warmed up quickly the man's foot would have to be cut off.

Then they had an idea. Lifting their woolly jumpers, they placed the man's frozen foot on their warm stomachs. Each man took his turn, though they could only bear the cold foot for a few minutes at a time. The warm stomachs helped bring the man's foot back to life.

Soon after, the awful Antarctic winter began to descend. Huddled together on board *Discovery*, the men knew that winter meant almost four months of total darkness for 24 hours a day, bitterly cold temperatures and vicious blizzards. Men rarely strayed from the ship in case they got lost in the blackness.

All thoughts turned to the spring, when the sun would return and slightly warmer weather would arrive. Spring also meant the men could mount a major sledging trek to explore the unknown continent.

The aim was to cross the vast, flat plain of ice which Shackleton had seen from the balloon. With luck they might even get them to the South Pole.

Captain Scott would lead a party of three men into the unknown. He chose his friend Bill Wilson and looked around for a third man. Shackleton, who was desperate for a chance to go exploring, pleaded to be allowed to go with him. Scott agreed and the three men set out on their historic march.

Their sledges pulled enough provisions to last the men for about three months and there were nineteen eager dogs to help. Flags were placed on the sledges and everyone hoped for a successful journey.

But Shackleton knew the risks. Danger was 'everywhere', he admitted.

Chapter 3

WHERE NO MAN STOOD BEFORE

The journey to the south, which began in early November 1902, was an ordeal from the start. Shackleton, Scott and Wilson struggled against strong winds and freezing temperatures.

The dogs, who were expected to help pull the sledge, soon became limp and tired. They were badly affected by the intense cold. As a result, the three men were forced to haul their own sledge, while the dogs walked alongside.

The wind was much stronger than expected and the bitter cold cut through their thick clothing and chilled them to the bone. Marching for hour after hour was exhausting. Often they sank up to their thighs in soft snow and on other occasions they slipped and fell heavily on the glassy ice.

Progress was very slow. They were new to ice travel and not good on skis. Sometimes the three men managed to cover only a few miles a day, despite backbreaking effort to drag the heavy sledge. Such hard work made them feel very hungry and they soon found their daily food rations were not enough. Each night after dinner they were still hungry.

Most of their food consisted of pemmican, a horrible blend of dried meat and fat which was mixed with biscuits or cheese and boiled in a pot. It produced a thick mushy porridge which the men called hoosh.

But the hoosh was not enough food for the hard-working men.

In the cold, windy conditions the men struggled badly. Things went from bad to worse when, one by one, the dogs began to die from the cold and lack of food.

Shackleton, too, was struggling. He was not in good health. He was very cold and hungry and soon developed a nasty cough. At night, he coughed so loudly that his companions were kept awake. Sometimes, he coughed up blood.

Wilson, who was a doctor, suspected scurvy, the dreadful complaint that is caused by a lack of vitamin C. People build up their vitamin C by eating fresh meat and vegetables. But there was nothing fresh in the hoosh they ate every night. Slowly, scurvy began to take a grip on the three explorers. Unless treated, scurvy is fatal.

Hungry, tired and cold, the men slogged on, day after day. At night they collapsed, exhausted in the tent. The situation called for drastic action.

It was decided to make the sledge lighter by leaving some food and equipment behind. The supplies were left in a carefully built depot which the men intended to pick up on the return journey to the ship. A cairn of snow was built over the food stock and a flag was stuck on top so the men would be able to spot the depot on their way back.

For almost eight weeks they marched on, feeling terribly cold and slowly getting weaker from hunger and the hard work of pulling the sledge. In the distance, a chain of mountains slowly began to come into view. This was the first time anyone had seen these towering peaks. Each day the mountains came closer.

The surviving dogs, too, were getting weaker and their food was running low. Only a handful of the animals now survived and they limped wearily alongside the men.

The only break the men had from the ordeal was on Christmas Day 1902 when, despite the terrible conditions, the three explorers enjoyed a mini feast.

Shackleton had another surprise for his companions – a tiny Christmas pudding which he secretly carried in the toe of a spare sock as a festive gift for the weary men. On top of the pudding was a sprig of fake holly to remind the men of Christmas at home.

Their Christmas feast was hoosh though, followed by a slice of Shackleton's Christmas pudding served with steaming hot cocoa. Crammed together in a little tent on the frozen land and hundreds of miles from any living person, it was their strangest Christmas dinner ever.

One of the nearby mountains was named Christmas Mountain in celebration. Shackleton scribbled in his diary: 'How strange and wild it is to be out here so many miles from all people.'

For another four days the men drove deeper into unknown territory, each day bringing the sight of new mountains looming into view. The only sounds were the crunching plod of footsteps breaking through the snow and the deep panting breaths of men straining to haul their heavy sledge. They rarely spoke.

Shackleton was very weak. It would not be long before Wilson and Scott fell ill too.

Continuing the march posed a huge risk. Unless they turned for home soon, the men might be too ill or too weak to get back to *Discovery*. On 30 December, almost two months after setting out, the group made their last camp.

But Scott wanted to push on, despite Shackleton's illness. In haste, Scott left Shackleton alone in the tent and drove on a few miles further south with Wilson. The extra miles set a new record for travelling to the most southerly spot ever reached by men.

Shackleton felt angry at being left behind. Alone in the tent, he fumed.

Shackleton, Scott and Wilson had walked almost 480km (300 miles) but the South Pole was still nearly 950km (600 miles) further away. It was impossible to continue the march.

Sadly they turned for home, anxious that their strength and supplies of food may not be enough to carry them back to the safety of *Discovery*.

It was very hard going. The men pulled in silence, always thinking about food. The dogs were a pitiful sight, thin and shaggy haired. Soon after this the last animals were put out of their misery.

Shackleton was also a pitiful sight. His strength had gone and he could not pull the sledge. He limped alongside his companions like a wounded animal. Wilson was worried Shackleton might not survive if the scurvy worsened.

Shackleton's condition went slowly downhill. Outside the tent one night, Scott and Wilson talked about Shackleton's desperate state. Wilson whispered gloomily that Shackleton would probably be dead within 24 hours.

But Shackleton overheard the shocking remark. He was no quitter. He resolved to fight back. He simply refused to die.

Somehow he found new strength and plodded on. It was a remarkable display of will-power and courage.

Luckily the men reached one of their supply depots and filled themselves with extra helpings of food. For the first time they sensed they would reach the safety of the ship.

Soon after, the three men came across the ski tracks of another sledging party, which meant they were close to the ship. A few days later they caught sight of two figures in the far distance hurrying towards them. In the whiteness of Antarctica's snow and ice, a person's dark clothing stands out sharply. It was their companions from *Discovery*. They made it!

The round trip of around 950km (600 miles) had taken three months of heavy slog. They had gone further south than anyone ever before. It was a new record. But the march nearly cost Shackleton his life.

The other explorers were shocked at the terrible state of the three men, particularly Shackleton. It was clear they had returned to the ship in the nick of time.

After a short recovery period, Shackleton was given a different kind of shock.

Captain Scott was worried about Shackleton's illness and took a severe step. He ordered Shackleton to leave the Antarctic and return home with a rescue ship which had arrived to bring fresh supplies to the explorers.

Shackleton was stunned and could hardly believe he was being rejected again. As the ship pulled away from the ice, Shackleton stood on deck waving farewell to his friends who were staying in the Antarctic for another year. Tears filled his eyes and rolled down his cheeks.

But Shackleton was a fighter. He resolved to come back to the Antarctic. Next time, he promised himself, he would be the boss and lead his own expedition.

Chapter 4

RETURN TO THE ICE

Shackleton kept his promise. Within a few years he had put together a plan to return to the Antarctic. This time he would be leader of his own expedition and his plan was bold and simple – to be the first man to reach the South Pole.

The expedition set sail in the summer of 1907 with high hopes of success. King Edward and Queen Alexandra of England came to see them off. The Queen gave Shackleton a special flag to plant at the South Pole.

Another special visitor was Emily, the woman Shackleton had married soon after coming home from the *Discovery* voyage. At her side were Raymond and Cecily, their two small children who would not see their father again for almost two years.

The wooden ship, called *Nimrod*, was loaded with supplies and equipment. Stacked on board was enough food for at least two years, plus sledges, tents and other vital gear for the march to the Pole.

The explorers took a sewing machine to mend clothes and various odds and ends like footballs, hockey sticks and a record player to play the latest hit tunes. Also on board was a typewriter and small printing press to produce their own newspaper in the Antarctic. But the oddest item was a motor car. Cars were a fairly new invention at the time and Shackleton's vehicle was the first car ever taken to the Antarctic. He thought the vehicle would be a great help dragging the heavy sledges across the ice. The car might be the key to reaching the Pole.

Shackleton's most prized items on board *Nimrod* though were a few huskies and ten white-haired ponies. The ponies were bought specially from the remote and cold region of Manchuria in China. He hoped their tough background would help them withstand the freezing conditions in the Antarctic.

The ship was so weighed down with animals and supplies that Shackleton had to get another ship to help tow the vessel on part of the journey.

It was a terrible trip, with hurricanes battering the ship and all the men horribly seasick in the wild waters. Sometimes the *Nimrod* completely disappeared behind the towering waves and sailors on the other ship thought the vessel had sunk without trace. One of the sailors declared the sea was so rough it would 'shake the milk out of your tea'.

Two of the ponies fell over and could not be lifted back onto their feet. Sadly, the poor beasts had to be shot. In contrast, one of the dogs gave birth to six puppies at the height of the storm.

Luckily the weather improved after a few days and the ships moved slowly towards the icy continent. When the first icebergs came into sight, the other ship cut the tow line between the two vessels and turned for home, leaving *Nimrod* to battle on alone. Five months after sailing from London, *Nimrod* finally reached the coast of Antarctica.

Stores, supplies and animals were quickly taken off the ship and the explorers built a wooden hut which was to be their home for the long Antarctic winter. When all the work was finished the *Nimrod* said goodbye and sailed back to the safety of warmer waters.

On the icy shore Shackleton and his fourteen men waved farewell and prepared to sit through the long, dark winter months. The green grass of New Zealand and the nearest human being was over 3,200km (2,000 miles) away.

The explorers used the winter months to prepare for the march to the South Pole the coming spring. There was much work to do, arranging supplies and equipment, building sledges and looking after the ponies and dogs.

The men also found time for a little fun. A magazine, called *Aurora Australis*, was produced on the printing press. At night they played cards, listened to records or read books.

Outside it was inky black and the wind howled non-stop. Sometimes the wooden hut shook from the battering winds.

In the fierce cold one of the men was struck by frostbite in the foot. The men tried to revive the man's limb. But they failed and the expedition's doctor was forced to cut off one of the man's big toes.

Another tragedy struck in the middle of the bleak winter. One day they noticed the ponies were sick. Before long four were dead, leaving only four ponies to make the long slog to the South Pole.

The odds were all against Shackleton reaching the Pole now.

Chapter 5

THE LONGEST MARCH

The South Pole, the very bottom of the earth, was almost 1,400km (900 miles) away, across land where no human had stood before. It would be hard to reach the Pole and harder still to get back. Even if he reached the Pole, Shackleton would be extremely tired and still have to face the same 1,400km trek to base camp.

Shackleton walked into the frozen wilderness in November 1908 with three other tough and reliable men. They were Frank Wild, Jameson Adams and Eric Marshall. To all the crew Shackleton was known as the Boss.

The Boss also took the four surviving ponies on the trek. The ponies – whose names were Chinaman, Socks, Grisi and Quan – were harnessed to heavy sledges piled up with food and equipment.

At first, the car began the journey and went along quite well, pulling very heavy loads of supplies. Hopes were high.

The car moved along fine while it was travelling over very hard ice. But the vehicle came to a grinding stop once it ran into soft, mushy snow. The wheels sank into the snow and could not turn properly.

Watching the scene in amusement was a group of Emperor penguins, who found the snow and ice perfectly ideal.

Soon after the car broke down one of the ponies went lame. Another kicked Adams, cutting his knee to the bone. Then a fierce blizzard struck and the men were confined to their tents for three days. Outside, in the bitter cold, the ponies shivered.

Despite the problems, Shackleton's expedition was travelling much faster than Scott managed on the *Discovery* expedition. Each day brought new sights as mountains never seen before slowly came into view. Before long they had beaten the record of 'furthest south' achieved by Shackleton, Scott and Wilson in 1902. All ahead was new land. The Pole was within reach.

But the march was taking a heavy toll on the poor, weak ponies. They were not suited to marching across the ice and snow. No one had taken ponies south before and they did not realise their hooves sank deep into the snow. Often they sank up to their bellies. Each step was a terrible strain.

Grisi collapsed and had to be put down. A few days later Quan, who was Shackleton's favourite pony, refused to move another step. He was shot as an act of kindness.

Chinaman, the oldest pony, had grown very weak through the heavy work. Within three weeks of starting the march, it was clear that Chinaman would not survive long. Soon he could not march any further. With a heavy heart, Shackleton had the animal shot. The horse meat was then stored for the men to eat on the return journey.

Only the sturdy Socks now remained alive. It was still 800km (500 miles) to the South Pole and almost 1,400km (900 miles) back to base – a daunting round trip of 2,250km (1,400 miles).

Shackleton summed up the isolation and sheer size of the march. He wrote in his diary: 'It seems as though we are truly at the world's end.'

But the hardest part of the journey was now ahead. Directly in their path lay a chain of mountains. They could not go round the peaks and knew the only way to the Pole was to climb one of them. The other alternative was to find a pass between the mountains.

After scouting the area, Shackleton found a way. Between two lines of mountains stood a giant glacier which rose steeply upwards. It looked like a giant children's slide – a vast sheet of treacherous ice sloping uphill towards the Pole.

Slowly the four men and Socks, the last surviving pony, edged towards the glacier and began the steep climb uphill. Shackleton named it the Beardmore Glacier, in honour of the businessman who had given him most of the money to pay for the expedition.

Climbing the mighty Beardmore Glacier was a terrifying prospect. The glacier, one of the world's largest, is 190km (120 miles) long and 23km (14 miles) wide. It moves about 1m (3ft) every day and is littered with dangerous and hidden crevasses, which could swallow a man and sledge in the blink of an eye.

The march up the Beardmore Glacier began with disaster. The ice was very hard and slippery and the men constantly fell over. Socks found it very hard to keep his footing. Danger was all around.

Wild, who was at the back of the march, suddenly let out a scream – 'Help!'

Shackleton, Adams and Marshall turned in alarm and ran towards Wild. They found him desperately clinging to the ice, his feet dangling into a vast gaping hole below. He was quickly dragged out.

The weak ice had collapsed under the weight of Wild and Socks. Luckily Wild had saved himself from falling down the crevasse. But Socks had disappeared.

The four men stood peering down into the deep black hole. There was no sign of the doomed Socks. Nor was there time to mourn the loss of the faithful pony. Or the loss of a fresh meat supply for the return march.

Day after day the march continued uphill in freezing temperatures and howling winds. It was very tiring work, dragging heavy sledges. Each night they ended their dinner wishing there was more hoosh in the pot.

As Christmas approached the explorers decided to have a celebration. A special Christmas dinner included plum pudding, brandy and cigars. It was a welcome break from the daily toil of pulling the heavy sledge up the glacier and eating grim hoosh for dinner. It was also the last time on the expedition that the men would feel full after their evening meal.

To help continue the march it was decided to reduce the weight of the sledges, which meant taking the drastic step of cutting down on food. Some of the food on the sledge was placed in a depot to be picked up on the return journey.

Progress was painfully slow. Shackleton wrote that 'everyone is weak' but they marched on and on. No one complained. The men pulled their sledge for ten hours a day, with only a short break for lunch. At the end of the march they collapsed, utterly exhausted, in their tent.

Towards the end of December the slope started to level off and the land ahead began to flatten out. They had finally reached the top of the Beardmore Glacier. Ahead lay around 480km (300 miles) of fairly flat ice to the South Pole.

On New Year's Eve, Shackleton did his sums. The South Pole was still around 320km (200 miles) away and food was running short. Once again it was decided to cut down on their daily rations of food and eat smaller meals. Seven day's food would have to stretch over ten days.

Each day's march was a terrible strain and at night they shivered with the cold and suffered pangs of hunger. Dinner was a mug of hoosh, two biscuits and a cup of tea – more a snack than a full meal after a day of heavy work.

The cold was intense. Marshall, the doctor in the group, took their body temperatures and was shocked to find a reading of 34.4°C (94°F) – the normal temperature for a healthy body is 37°C (98.4°F).

The weather became much worse as the new year of 1909 arrived. Winds shrieked loudly, roaring to 80 mph at times. The explorers could barely stand the cold. The temperature dropped to a bone-chilling -30°C (-25°F). One man said he felt paralysed with the cold. Shackleton was so cold at night he could not write up his diary, even when tucked up in a thick sleeping bag. Shivering in his bag,

Shackleton pondered the future. Should he abandon the march so near the Pole and turn for home?

The men had already achieved a record march of over 1,200km (750 miles). It was an incredible feat of courage and endurance. And the Boss had to consider the safety of his men.

Shackleton once again did his sums. He calculated the four men had just enough food to reach the South Pole.

But there was not enough food on the sledge to get back to the safety of base camp. Death was certain if they continued the march south.

'We have shot our bolt,' he wrote in his diary.

Shackleton wanted to be a famous hero. Getting to the South Pole would make him the greatest living explorer of the age. But what good is a dead hero?

Shackleton also knew that his men trusted him. He had taken them to the ends of the earth and vowed to get them back. So Shackleton stopped the march and turned for home.

Shackleton marked the spot by taking photographs of the men. The flag, which Queen Alexandra had given him, flew stiffly in the strong wind. They were barely 179km (112 statute miles or 97 geographic miles) from the South Pole – the furthest point south ever reached by humans. So near, yet so far.

Shackleton was very disappointed not to have fulfilled his dream of reaching the Pole. But he put the lives of his men first. 'We have done all we could,' he said.

Shackleton later told his wife, Emily: 'I thought you would prefer a live donkey to a dead lion.'

It was a very brave decision to abandon the march when so close to the South Pole. And it certainly took more courage to call off the march than to carry on.

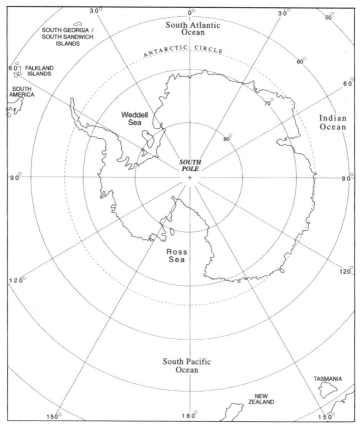

The Antarctic: the fifth largest continent was largely unexplored at the start of the twentieth century.

Chapter 6

MARCH OR DIE

Shackleton, Wild, Adams and Marshall stayed only a few minutes at the spot which marked their record 'furthest south'. It was too cold to linger.

Temperatures had dropped to nearly -30°C (-22°F) and the wind cut through their clothing. Frostbite nipped at their faces.

Nor could they afford to waste time. The march back to base camp, a distance of over 1,200km (750 miles), was a massive task. But the four explorers had no choice – it was march or die in their tracks.

The journey started fairly well and the men made good distances. On one day they covered over 40km (26 miles), helped by a strong wind blowing at their back. The men rigged up a sail on the sledge and were blown along by the wind, like a sailing ship at sea.

The most vital task was to find the depots of food left on the outward march. The food depots were the difference between life and death. If they failed to find the depots, they would starve to death.

The good start helped to lift the four men's spirits. Soon they had reached the top of the Beardmore Glacier, where they found their precious depot of food. They gulped down a good, solid meal, which made them feel better to face the challenge ahead. Slowly the men began to climb down the huge glacier. They moved carefully, anxious not to stand on any weak ice and fall down a hidden crevasse like poor old Socks. Often they slipped and fell heavily on the hard ice. But no one was lost.

The next target was the food depot built near the bottom of the Beardmore Glacier, about 160km (100 miles) away. It was essential they reach this before their food ran out.

Hurrying along as fast as possible, the four made good progress. Food was very low when, to their utter relief, the black flag fluttering on top of the vital depot was finally spotted.

There was no time to waste. After a fine meal and a good night's sleep, the four men set off again.

Once they marched from 7 o'clock in the morning until 9 o'clock at night, frantic to cover as many miles as possible before the food was all gone. Dinner was a miserable mug of hoosh and one solitary biscuit. It was still about 65km (40 miles) to the depot.

They marched on, getting more tired and hungry by the day. The men ate their last meal, a mug of hoosh made from pony feed and a cup of steaming-hot tea. All that remained for lunch was a tiny 30gm (1 oz) piece of chocolate.

But the depot was nowhere in sight. The men strained their eyes for the black flag on top of it. It was nowhere to be seen.

All four men were close to collapse. On one day, it took them an hour to walk only 800m (875yds) over very broken ground. Fit and well-fed men would easily walk 800m in a matter of minutes. Only will-power was driving them on.

Once the worn-out Adams lay down in the snow and pleaded for Shackleton to allow him to sleep for 30 minutes. 'Only half a hour,' he begged. But Shackleton knew Adams would freeze to death if he slept in the very low temperatures.

Adams curled up on the ground and closed his eyes. Shackleton waited a few moments until he dropped off. He then kicked him in the backside to wake him. He told Adams to get up because he had been asleep for half an hour. He had to be cruel to be kind.

Shackleton worked out that the depot was quite near. But they were too weak to continue. So they set up camp for a rest.

However, Marshall, the doctor, knew better than anyone that the men needed hot food urgently. They had not eaten properly for two days. The men were all close to collapse. Marshall feared they might all die soon without food.

He bravely volunteered to go on alone to find the depot and bring back food for his starving friends. Luckily, he found the vital depot after about 30 minutes. However, on the return journey, Marshall only just escaped plunging to his death down a crevasse. He returned clutching horsemeat and pemmican for the hoosh, as well as some tea, biscuits and sugar. It was a feast.

Next day, the men reached the bottom of the Beardmore Glacier. Soon after, a blizzard struck the area, making it impossible to see ahead. They would never have found the depot had the blizzard struck a day earlier.

Helped by the warming food, the men started the last leg of the journey. It was still 640km (400 miles) to base camp but the ice was mostly hard and flat. Travel would be easier.

The next target was a depot 80km (50 miles) away. They had six days' food on the sledge, which meant they had to cover at least 13km (8 miles) a day to reach the depot.

But bad luck struck soon after they began their march. Wild became ill. The horsemeat and hoosh had made him sick. The only food he could swallow was dry biscuits. Shackleton knew that without proper food Wild would soon become weak and die.

Shackleton then showed his great kindness. He gave Wild his last biscuit, despite his own intense hunger. It was an act of sacrifice that only a starving man could fully grasp.

Soon after, the four men managed to stumble back to the depot where they enjoyed a decent feed. It revived them for the next leg of the journey.

The next depot, which contained more chunks of frozen horsemeat, was about 100km (60 miles) away. But they had only enough food for five days. It meant walking at least 20km (12 miles) a day. It was a major effort for tired men.

Often they walked for eleven hours a day, rarely stopping for a rest. It was freezing and a strong wind was blowing. Dinner was a few scraps of frozen horsemeat, biscuits and tea. Each man was gripped by the thought of food and at night they dreamed of eating feasts. Shackleton's dream was of sizzling bacon and fried eggs.

Somehow the weary men made it to the depot. After feeding themselves and resting, they set out again. On they marched, fighting the cold and hunger. They were thin, filthy dirty and their beards had grown long and straggly. Their bones ached and the bitterly cold wind showed no mercy.

Shackleton was so weak he barely had the strength to scribble a few lines in his diary. One night he wrote: 'Outlook serious' and another night the only words he could write were, 'Terribly hungry'. Later he wrote a gloomy warning: 'Our food lies ahead and death stalks us from behind.'

The trek was now a terrible ordeal. The men marched in total silence. When they eventually came across the depot the relief was enormous. After scraping away the snow covering the depot, the men found a welcome bonus. Inside was some horse liver, which made a welcome change from the normal hoosh diet. They also came across chunks of dried blood, frozen solid in the snow. The blood drops were quickly cut from the ice and thrown in the pot to make a boiling hot soup.

Once again, the men felt stronger after a good feed. But food was still very short and the next depot was about 130km (80 miles) away. A full day's march still brought only a tiny reward at dinner-time – a few slices of horsemeat and four biscuits.

On they marched, day after day. But a juicy little windfall greeted them at the next supply depot. Inside, they found enough biscuits and jam to make a pudding. Boosted by the extra helpings of food, the four men started off to find the next depot, which was about three days away.

But the cruel Antarctic weather began to close in. Winds grew stronger and the temperature dropped to -37°C (-35°F). The cold sliced through their clothes and chilled them to the bone.

The group should have camped to wait for better weather. But with food low and their strength failing, the four men had to march on. The alternative was death.

It was a terrible march. But their hopes were raised when they came across some ski and dog tracks which had been left on the ice by their companions a few days earlier. It meant they were near base camp.

The sight of the tracks lifted their spirits and they soon reached the vital food depot. They only had a few biscuits left.

Shackleton said the depot was the 'most cheerful sight our eyes have ever seen'. Inside was a well-stocked larder including sausages and helpings of porridge. To his joy, Shackleton also found some eggs.

The men tucked in. But without thinking, they ate too much. After months of starvation, their bodies were not used to rich and good food. Marshall became very ill. He was too sick to walk any further and the base-camp hut was still a good distance away.

The expedition ship, *Nimrod*, was due to depart from the Antarctic in a few days. *Nimrod* could not stay long in case the winter ice trapped the ship and blocked off their escape from the continent.

Shackleton was desperate to alert the ship. If *Nimrod* left without them, the explorers would be stranded on the ice. Missing the ship and spending a year alone, in the wilderness of Antarctica was too horrible to consider.

Shackleton had to make a tough decision. He decided to leave Adams behind in the tent to nurse the sick Marshall. He would dash to base camp with Wild, who had recovered from his own illness. From the base hut Shackleton and Wild hoped to send a signal to *Nimrod*.

It was about 50km (32 miles) to the expedition's hut and Shackleton and Wild walked as quickly as their very tired bodies would allow. But in their rush to catch the ship they made the mistake of packing only enough food for one meal.

Shackleton and Wild walked for 36 hours – a day and a half – with only a brief stop to eat their small rations. The two men called on their last reserves of strength.

It was getting dark as the two tired men finally staggered into the little hut. No one was inside and there was alarming news.

One of Shackleton's men had left a note reporting that *Nimrod* would wait for them in nearby waters only until 26 February. The date today was 28 February. Shackleton was shocked. *Nimrod* had gone without them!

Many of the other explorers at the base hut had given up hope of seeing Shackleton again. All logic said the Boss must be dead. For the men at base camp, the facts were simple. The four explorers had taken enough food for a march of 91 days. By the end of February, the group had been on the march for 120 days – almost a month longer than expected.

Shackleton and Wild climbed to the top of a nearby hill, hoping to see *Nimrod* moored offshore. But disappointment awaited them. There was no sign of the ship. *Nimrod* must have sailed!

The one slim chance was that the ship was not too far away. Shackleton decided to send a signal and hope it would be spotted by the crew on the *Nimrod.*

A flare was fired but there was no response. *Nimrod's* crew did not spot the signal. In desperation they found a small wooden shed and broke it up to make a bonfire. But the wood was damp and refused to catch light. Next a flag was found but Shackleton and Wild's hands were so cold they could not tie it to the flagpole.

Hopes of rescue soared when Shackleton saw a small group of dark figures far away in the distance. He thought the shapes were men moving slowly towards the hut. But the 'men' turned out to be a small group of penguins shuffling along.

Next a mirror was found to catch the sun's reflection and flash signals out to sea. It was their last hope.

Shackleton stood on the hill flashing the mirror. Suddenly smoke appeared on the horizon. It was the ship. They had been spotted.

Before long *Nimrod* sailed slowly into view. Shackleton flashed another signal and the ship turned towards the shore. They had done it!

Not long after, Shackleton and Wild were on board *Nimrod*. They celebrated the rescue with Shackleton's favourite meal – a hearty plate of bacon and eggs. It was a feast fit for kings.

After a good feed, Shackleton went back onto the ice with three others and rescued Adams and the sick Marshall. All four were soon back together on board *Nimrod*.

The journey had taken a heavy toll on the men. They were a terrible sight – thin, scraggy, filthy dirty and utterly worn out. They had barely survived.

But Shackleton, Wild, Adams and Marshall had been further south than anyone before. They had stood only 179km (112 miles) from the South Pole.

It was a great triumph. For Shackleton, it was almost the fulfilment of his boyhood dreams. But he wanted more.

Once again, Shackleton promised himself he would return to the ice.

Chapter 7

A FAMOUS MAN

When he came home in 1909 Shackleton had become a major celebrity. Crowds flocked to the streets just to catch a glimpse of the famous explorer. Police were called in to control the crush.

King Edward and Queen Alexandra, who had given Shackleton's *Nimrod* expedition a royal send-off two years earlier, called him to Buckingham Palace to honour him with a knighthood for his great feat in getting so close to the South Pole.

People everywhere wanted to see Shackleton and hear about his exploits at the end of the earth. He travelled widely and met the most powerful men in the world – the American President, the German Kaiser and Russian Tsar.

Tsar Nicolas of Russia was gripped by Shackleton's tale of adventure and survival in the Antarctic. It was intended that Shackleton should meet the Russian ruler at the famous Winter Palace for only fifteen minutes. But the Tsar was so spellbound he kept him chatting for over two hours.

Shackleton enjoyed the fame. But he was restless. The call of the frozen wilderness remained very strong. He wanted adventure. The dream of reaching the South Pole was just as strong. He was

determined to mount another expedition.

Shackleton was the sort of man who found ordinary day-to-day life dull and boring. He was only happy when sailing the seas or marching across the ice.

However, Shackleton did not have the white continent to himself. Other explorers had their own plans to reach the South Pole.

Shackleton's biggest rival was Captain Scott, leader of the *Discovery* expedition. Scott also had a burning ambition to stand at the Pole. As soon as Shackleton came home from the *Nimrod* voyage, Scott launched his own bid to reach the Pole.

Unknown to either Shackleton or Scott, however, another explorer was quietly plotting to capture the prize of being first at the South Pole.

He was Roald Amundsen from Norway. Amundsen was the world's most skilled explorer of the ice and snow. He turned his attention to the South Pole after he was beaten in the race to reach the North Pole.

Amundsen and Captain Scott set off in the same year, racing each other to stand first at the South Pole. Amundsen, using teams of strong husky dogs, won the race in December 1911.

It was a great feat of exploration but it was soon overshadowed by tragedy. Captain Scott and his four comrades arrived at the South Pole only one month after Amundsen.

But disaster struck Scott's party and all five died of cold and hunger on the return march. Amundsen's great triumph and Scott's terrible disaster stunned Shackleton. Robbed of the chance to be the first at the Pole, Shackleton searched for a new plan. It did not take Shackleton long to announce a bold new expedition.

His grand plan was to walk across the vast white continent from sea to sea. It was a massive trek of more than 2,800km (1,800 miles), a journey never attempted before.

It turned out to be the greatest adventure story in the history of Antarctic exploration.

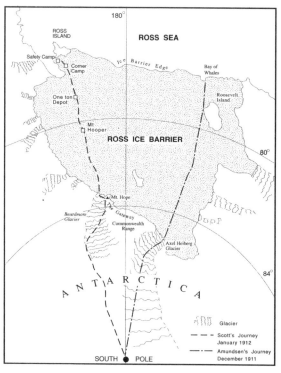

The route to the Pole: Amundsen and Scott's tracks on their 1,800-mile journeys in 1911-12.

Chapter 8

TRAPPED!

Thousands of men were eager to join Shackleton's expedition to cross Antarctica. Despite the dangers, poor wages and freezing cold conditions, about 5,000 men asked to join the Boss on his new adventure.

The expedition sailed from London in August 1914, just a few days before the First World War started. On board were tons of supplies for a journey of two years, about 60 husky dogs and a band of strong, willing men Shackleton knew he could trust.

Shackleton's men were a tough lot. They included the trusty Frank Wild from the *Nimrod* expedition and Tom Crean, the robust Irishman who travelled on *Discovery* and had survived Captain Scott's doomed South Pole expedition.

The expedition ship was a wooden vessel called *Endurance*. It was *Endurance's* first ever voyage.

The crew of the *Endurance* had their first surprise soon after departure. It was Tom Crean who discovered something strange – a pair of legs sticking out from the bottom of a weather-proof jacket hanging on the wall.

Tom stuck his hand under the jacket and found the legs were attached to a young man – a stowaway, a nineteen-year-old seaman called Percy Blackborrow.

Shackleton knew it was too late to turn *Endurance* round and take Blackborrow back to shore. But he had another idea.

He explained to the stowaway that life was very tough on Polar expeditions. He told Blackborrow about the *Discovery* and *Nimrod* expeditions, when the men almost starved to death. Sometimes, he said, the men were forced to eat anything they could find.

'And if anyone has to be eaten,' he joked, 'you will be first!'

Endurance had to make one last stop for supplies before entering the icy waters around the Antarctic Continent. The last port of call was South Georgia, the small island in the South Atlantic Ocean beyond the tip of South America, which was home to fleets of whaling ships.

Shackleton had another reason to stop at South Georgia. He wanted to ask the whaling captains about the state of the ice. The news was not good.

The sea captains, who spent most of their time hunting whales in the cold Antarctic seas, gloomily warned that the ice that year was very bad. It was far thicker than normal. The whalers could not remember a worse year for ice and they warned Shackleton not to risk *Endurance* getting trapped.

Shackleton listened quietly. Reaching the Antarctic coast meant guiding *Endurance* through more than 2,000km (1,200 miles) of treacherous ice in the Weddell Sea.

The Weddell Sea is one of the most fearsome stretches of water on earth. The sea is a graveyard for ships. Even today, modern ice-breakers very rarely stray into the dangerous waters where the ice is thick, and unforgiving. It can crush a ship like a matchbox.

Shackleton faced a difficult choice – either abandon the expedition or take their chances on the Weddell Sea. Shackleton, the fighter, decided to tackle the Weddell.

Endurance pulled away from South Georgia in December 1914. On board were 28 men hoping for a successful voyage. For a moment, the warnings from the whalers were forgotten.

Three days after leaving South Georgia the first icebergs came into view. Everyone was surprised to see ice so soon. It meant that the seas were colder and more dangerous than expected. The whalers' warnings were right.

Endurance dodged and weaved through the crooked network of ice. Often the ship had to ram the ice to break through to safer waters. Sometimes *Endurance* steered around the larger bergs. Luckily they found enough open lanes of water for the ship to pick a pathway to the south.

The ship made good progress, despite the maze of ice. From the crow's nest at the top of the ship sailors could see faint outlines of mountains in the far distance. The continent was within striking distance. With luck, the explorers would be on dry land in a matter of days.

But luck did not last long.

The ship's target was a small bay on the Antarctic coastline, where Shackleton hoped to build a hut as a base camp before embarking on the march across the continent. By now the bay was only 120 km (75 miles) away and the weather was quite good.

But the nearer *Endurance* came to the coast, the worse the ice seemed to get. Finding lanes of open water became more tricky. Soon it was almost impossible. Slowly the open lanes began to freeze over and disappear. The ice of the Weddell Sea began to close in around *Endurance*.

At first no one was too worried. Some expected that the strong wind and currents would soon carry the ice away.

The problem was the direction of the powerful winds. They came from behind the ship and drove the ice towards the Antarctic mainland. *Endurance* was caught in the middle. With no channels of open sea to allow the ship to escape, *Endurance* was trapped, unable to move.

No one was sure how long the ship would remain stuck in the ice. But one gloomy sailor remembered the old saying – 'What the ice gets, the ice keeps'.

Shackleton waited, hoping the ice would release its grip. From the crow's nest, land was now clearly visible, just 100km (60 miles) across the ice. In normal, open waters, the bay where they planned to build the base hut was little more than a good day's sailing away.

But the ice had no intention of letting go. Days passed, then weeks.

Still *Endurance* was stuck fast.

The ship was moving very slowly. Strong currents in the Weddell Sea carried the ice along and *Endurance* was also being swept along, unable to steer.

Before long the trapped ship was carried past the bay where Shackleton wanted to build his base camp. The crew could only watch. A few days later the bay disappeared from view altogether and the chance of landing on the continent had gone. The *Endurance* was at the mercy of the currents.

What is more, *Endurance* had no radio to signal for help and the men could not expect to be rescued from another ship because no other vessels dared to venture into the nasty Weddell Sea. The nearest human was at least 2,000km (1,200 miles) away in South Georgia.

Shackleton and his men were cut off and surrounded by an endless ocean of hostile ice. And no one would come to the rescue.

Chapter 9

CRUSHED

Shackleton feared the worst for *Endurance*. But the Boss did not tell his men that the expedition was doomed. Sailors dread the loss of their ship more than anything else. He did not want them to lose hope.

Endurance's only hope was the direction of the sea's currents. The currents in the Weddell Sea move around in a circle, like the hour hand on a giant clock. They start at '1 o'clock' in the north and flow south to '6 o'clock' in the south before turning upwards towards '12 midnight'. Then the process starts all over again.

If the currents carried the ship northwards to warmer waters, the ice would break up and the ship could find a path to open sea.

But it might take months, even a year to drift north and break free from the ice. Shackleton knew this and he prepared his men for the dark Antarctic winter.

The sun disappears for months during the winter there and some found it difficult to live in total darkness for 24 hours a day. Only a few men on board, like Tom Crean and Frank Wild, had previously experienced the bleak, cold winter so it was important to get everyone ready for it.

Shackleton tried to keep the men busy. He thought that if the men had lots of jobs to do and time for a few games it would take their minds off the desperate situation they were in.

Some men were sent out onto the ice to shoot seals or penguins for the cooking pot. Others kept themselves busy with mending clothes or preparing equipment for the sledges.

Shackleton took special care of the 60 huskies on board *Endurance*. They were taken off the ship and placed in kennels built out of ice, which the men called a 'dogloo'.

The dogs were then put into six different teams in readiness for sledging expeditions. Each dog had its own name: Bob, Jerry, Mack, Martin, Noel, Paddy, Roy, Rufus, Soldier, Sooty, Steamer, Sue, Surly, Wolf and Samson, the largest of all.

Sally, one of Tom Crean's dogs, had four puppies and before long Tom was out on the ice training the little dogs to pull a sledge. He shouted 'Mush' to start the team moving and 'Ha' meant turn left. To turn right Tom shouted 'Gee' and to stop he yelled 'Whoa'. He named the pups Roger, Toby, Nell and Nelson.

Once, they had a race between the six dog teams. The men placed bets on who would win, betting cigarettes or tobacco instead of hard cash. Frank Wild's team won.

Another favourite of the men was the ship's cat. The cat belonged to the ship's carpenter, Chippy McNish, and was called Mrs Chippy. This was odd because Mrs Chippy was a male cat, but no one discovered this until after Mrs Chippy got his name.

While there was still enough light the men often played games of football on the ice. Pitches were marked out and goal posts stuck in the ice. It was bitterly cold and there was plenty of sliding tackles. One team wore red arm bands and the other white.

At night the men read books and enjoyed games of cards and chess, or a match on the ship's mini-snooker table. Often they had a sing-song, helped by the record player or by one of the crew who had brought his banjo on the expedition.

Food was the biggest concern. A group of 28 men eat a huge amount of food every day and hunting parties were always busy. Each day, they took to the ice looking for fresh stocks of seals and penguins.

Seals were very valuable. The flesh was fried like a steak and the fatty blubber could be boiled to make oil for the stoves and lamps.

There was little fish to eat, as the men were very poor at catching fish, except on one occasion.

One day, a sailor took a walk on the ice and wandered away from the ship. Suddenly a giant sea leopard, which is about 3m (10ft) in length, broke through the ice and tried to attack the sailor. Luckily, Frank Wild saw the sea leopard and quickly shot the beast with his rifle before it could hurt the sailor.

When the sea leopard was gutted, the men found undigested fish in the beast's stomach. That night, the men had 'fresh' fish to go with their main course of sea leopard steaks.

All the while the powerful currents were carrying the *Endurance* slowly north towards warmer waters. February, March and April passed and then May, June and July. By August, the ship had drifted about 1,300 km (800 miles). It was eight months since *Endurance* first became trapped.

But the currents and the warmer waters towards the north began to disturb the ice. It started to break up. Huge ice-floes began to grind and press against each other. Some ice got caught underneath *Endurance*.

The movement of the ice posed a grave danger to *Endurance*. *Endurance* was caught, unable to steer out of danger, as the huge slabs of ice stirred and rubbed against each other. Shackleton knew that the ship would be crushed unless *Endurance* could escape.

The grinding of the ice began to get louder and louder. At night, the men sat silently in their bunks listening to the rumbling sounds of the moving ice. It sounded like distant thunder.

Soon the ship began to buckle under the strain of the moving ice. Timbers groaned and strained from the pressure. Some planks began to split, and hefty beams buckled and snapped like matchsticks. Water began to pour into the ship.

Ice started to move underneath the ship as the *Endurance* was pushed out of the water. Soon the vessel tipped over at a crazy angle, half out of the water and half in. *Endurance* was doomed unless the ship could be re-floated in open water.

Shackleton knew the end was in sight. He ordered the men to start pumping out the water. But he also began preparing for the grim task of abandoning *Endurance*.

Food, equipment and anything else of value was first taken off the ship, including the three lifeboats. Tents were put up on the ice, and the men tried to make themselves comfortable. Special 'dogloos' were built for the dogs.

On board the ship, planks and beams snapped and split and water gushed in. The water poured in faster than the men could pump it out. Shackleton said that no ship built of human hands could have withstood the strain from the pressure of the ice. The end was near.

Towards the end of October, exactly ten months after *Endurance* had first become trapped in the ice, the Boss called the men together on the ice. Behind them *Endurance* was a broken hulk, waiting to sink.

The men were anxious, the food stock was poor, the dogs were yelping and equipment was scattered all over the ice. No one in the outside world knew the fate of *Endurance* and no search parties were out looking for the men.

The ice where the men stood was only about 2m (6 ft) thick, and beneath that the sea was 3.5km (2 miles) deep. The nearest land was around 400km (250 miles) away, across broken, heaving ice floes. But this land was uninhabited and remote.

The situation was desperate. But Shackleton was a fighter who refused to give up. He wanted to show his men they would survive – despite the odds stacked against them. And the men trusted the Boss.

'So now we'll go home, boys,' a defiant Boss declared.

Chapter 10

MAROONED

No one slept very well in the tents that first night on the ice. The constant rumbling of the ice and the biting cold kept them awake. The men could also hear the eerie sounds in the darkness as planks splintered and snapped on the stricken *Endurance*, barely 100m (90 yards) away.

At the back of everyone's mind was the knowledge that the cold, deep ocean lay beneath the tent floor-cloth. And the strong currents of the Weddell Sea were still carrying the men further north into unknown waters.

Shackleton barely slept at all. He was thinking about how to save his men.

By the morning, Shackleton had drawn up a plan of escape. The Boss called all hands together and told the men how they would break free from the icy prison.

The idea was to march across the ice-floes to a little place called Paulet Island at the tip of Antarctica. The island was around 650km (400 miles) away. Shackleton knew there was a wooden hut on Paulet Island stocked with food and supplies in case of emergencies.

They would need great courage and much luck if they were to reach Paulet Island. The march would also mean making big sacrifices.

They would have to carry all their food and equipment on the march. There would be no room for extra items or luxuries.

The Boss led by example. Each man was allowed to take only 900gm (2lbs) of personal items on the march. He stood up in front of the men and emptied his pockets. Shackleton took out his gold watch and some money. After a last look, he tossed them onto the ice.

All the men followed his example. Soon the ice was littered with coins, spare clothes, odd items of equipment and piles of books. Only one luxury item was kept. Shackleton ordered that the banjo be kept so the men could enjoy a sing-song at night.

Even the ship's Bible was thrown away. But a cautious sailor picked it up and tucked it under his jumper when no one was looking. The sailor believed throwing a Bible away would bring bad luck.

What to do with the animals was the toughest decision Shackleton was forced to make. There was only enough food for the strongest dogs who could pull sledges. There was no room for passengers and those too weak to pull had to be put down.

The same fate awaited Mrs Chippy, the ship's cat. Food was not the problem, since cats do not eat very much. But Shackleton was worried that the dogs would attack the little cat when their own food ran low. It was an act of kindness to put her down, though it made the men very sad.

Shackleton's survival plan involved placing the lifeboats on sledges and dragging them across the ice. Dog teams would pull other sledges. If the ice broke up on the way, the men would get in the lifeboats and sail towards land.

However, the boats were very heavy. Each boat weighed around 1,000kg (1 ton) and needed fifteen strong men to drag it along.

The strain on the men was huge. Hour after hour they plodded along, dragging their heavy boats. They could only manage a few hundred metres before sinking to their knees on the ice, gasping for breath.

The men made very little progress, despite the hard and tiring work. At the end of the first day's exhausting march it was calculated that the parade of men, boats, sledges and dog teams had travelled only 1.6km (1 mile).

At this rate of progress, it would take almost a year to reach Paulet Island. None of the men would survive that long. Next day, Shackleton abandoned the hopeless march.

A new camp was built on the floating ice. He called it Ocean Camp. The 28 men lived for seven weeks at Ocean Camp. It was very boring, but the ice was firmer and the men a little safer than before.

The saddest moment came with the final crushing end of *Endurance*. Ocean Camp was not far from the ship and the men watched, day by day, as the ice began to squeeze the life out of the vessel. By late November, only 6m (20ft) of the ship's rear end could be seen sticking out of the water.

One night, shortly before darkness, Shackleton called his men together and they stood in silence, watching as *Endurance* slipped quietly beneath the ice and disappeared, forever. It was the end of *Endurance's* first and only voyage.

Weeks passed with the men waiting patiently at Ocean Camp. Shortly before Christmas, Shackleton noticed the ice was beginning to break up. Odd patches of open water were seen. It meant that the powerful currents were still carrying the Ocean Camp ice-floe into warmer waters.

But the drift carried another big risk for Shackleton. There was a danger that the currents would carry the men too far from land and out into the vast Southern Ocean, between the continents of South America and South Africa. There is no land in the wide ocean between the two continents and the 28 men would be doomed.

Shackleton sensed the time was right to make a new march to reach land, before the drift took them into the open ocean. The boats were loaded, sledges packed and the men had a last feast. All the food not packed on the sledges was gobbled up.

Next day, the march began. It was another ordeal for the men who strained and struggled all day, dragging the heavy boats over the jumble of broken and lumpy ice. But it was another waste of time and effort.

The men travelled only a few kilometres in a day, but land was hundreds of kilometres away across the ice. After only a few days of terrible toil, the march was stopped.

A new camp was built. This time they named it Patience Camp, because the men knew they would have to wait for days, weeks and possibly months for the currents to carry them north. Only when they reached warmer waters in the north could they launch the lifeboats.

The new year of 1916 arrived with the men stuck at Patience Camp, drifting slowly north. 'May the new year bring us good fortune,' Shackleton wrote in his diary.

Weeks passed, then months. January gave way to February and March. All the time, the men sat and waited. Often, they ventured onto the ice to shoot penguins and seals for food. But mostly life was very boring.

Shackleton summed up the position. In his diary one night he simply wrote: 'Waiting. Waiting. Waiting.'

But Shackleton never let the men get downhearted or depressed. Every day he told them they would definitely survive. The Boss gave them hope.

By April, the ice-floe containing Patience Camp had begun to break up. The warmer waters were starting to eat into the floe. It was slushy and messy underfoot. The ice was slowly melting. Before long the floe would melt altogether. The time to launch the lifeboats was getting near.

The drift of the floe had taken the men nearer to Paulet Island. Across the horizon, the island was perhaps only 100km (60 miles) away. But the jumble of broken ice was far too difficult to cross, hauling the heavy lifeboats.

They would have a faint hope of sailing to safety, if they built a larger boat. A wooden church stood on one of the nearby islands, and it was suggested that the building should be smashed up and the wood used to make a large boat. But the march across the ice to the church was not safe and the idea was rejected.

It was a very frustrating time. Slowly, the ice-floe drifted north towards the very end of the Weddell Sea. At one stage they could see the tops of far away mountains. But the currents carried them onwards. Each day they drifted further from the land.

The land was left behind and the floe, which had grown very small, was now in warmer waters. For the first time in well over a year, the explorers felt the swell of the seas beneath their feet. Open water was not far away.

Shackleton said it was time to make a move. Food was running low and the last of the dogs, who could not be taken on the boats, were sadly put down. The men prepared for the sea voyage.

At night the men slept with their clothes and boots on in case the floe broke up completely. They had to be ready to dash for the boats in 30 seconds flat.

To the north, about 160km (100 miles) away, lay two small islands. These were Clarence Island and Elephant Island. When the time came to launch the boats, these islands would be their target.

While they waited the men were given a stark warning. The floe split in half, leaving one of the lifeboats marooned on one chunk of ice and all the rest on Patience Camp. The lifeboat was quickly rescued and all three boats were loaded and made ready to sail. Another split in the floe could be fatal. There was no time to lose.

On 9 April 1916 Shackleton ordered the men to eat a hearty breakfast. All three lifeboats were dragged to the ice edge and the men waited for clear lanes of water to appear. At lunchtime, they got their wish. Channels of open water, large enough to take the lifeboats, slowly came into sight.

At 1 o'clock in the afternoon Shackleton ordered the three small boats into the water. The 28 men and boxes of food and equipment were packed tightly into the vessels. They said goodbye to Patience Camp and headed for land.

The 28 men had been stuck on the ice for fifteen months and travelled around 3,200km (2,000 miles) in a giant semi-circle around the Weddell Sea since *Endurance* first became trapped. But the toughest part of their ordeal lay ahead.

Chapter 11

A BOAT RIDE TO HELL

The three little lifeboats were a sorry sight, surrounded by giant icebergs and chunks of floating ice. Any collision would sink a boat and the men would freeze to death in the icy cold waters.

Only a few channels of open water were visible between the lumps of ice. But after fifteen months drifting at the mercy of the currents, Shackleton was glad to be at sea once again.

The odds of finding Clarence or Elephant Island were very small. It would be a miracle if all 28 survived the journey. The rough seas and menacing ice were bad enough. But the men also had to overcome exhaustion, hunger and the bitterly cold weather.

All three vessels sat low in the water because they were packed with men, food and equipment. Waves splashed over the sides and soaked the men. Some rowed while others bailed out the water which poured over the sides with every passing wave.

Shackleton took the lead and stood up at the back of the largest boat, using the rudder to steer a path through the ice. He named his lifeboat the *James Caird* after the rich businessman who had given the most money towards the cost of the expedition. The other boats were called *Dudley Docker* and *Stancomb Wills* after two other supporters of the expedition.

Rowing was very tiring, particularly as the men were not used to hard work after months sitting around on the drifting ice-floe. As night began to fall Shackleton saw that his men were utterly drained. He steered the boats towards a large ice-floe where a camp was set up and the cooking stove was fired up.

Tents were erected and a hot dinner was cooked. Soon the men scrambled into their sleeping bags and settled down for a well-earned rest.

But Shackleton was restless, unable to sleep. He felt something was wrong. Late at night, in pitch darkness, he suddenly leapt from his sleeping bag and went out to inspect the state of the ice-floe.

As Shackleton walked along, the ice split open underneath one of the tents. The crack in the ice was over 1m (3ft) wide and Shackleton heard a desperate call for help in the darkness. He rushed forward and saw that one of the sailors had fallen into the freezing water. The sailor was kicking and struggling to get out of his sleeping bag before the weight dragged him under.

In an instant, Shackleton thrust his hand into the icy sea, grabbed the man and yanked him out of the water. The sailor was soaked but safe. When Shackleton asked if he was OK, the sailor's only concern was that his tobacco had got wet.

But Shackleton was marooned by the split in the ice-floe. His men were on one large floe. He was drifting out to sea on the smaller chunk of ice. The *Stancomb Wills* was promptly launched and Shackleton picked off the floe before the currents carried him out to sea.

No one slept another wink. The men sat up all night, shivering with the cold and fearful that another crack in the ice would send them toppling into the freezing water.

The wet sailor was in the worst state. There were no dry clothes available and he was bitterly cold. If he sat down too long his wet clothes would freeze solid like a suit of armour. His pals took turns throughout the long night to walk him up and down on the ice. As long as he kept moving, the sailor's clothes would not freeze and he would stay alive.

When dawn broke the men launched the boats and set off again. Led by Shackleton's *James Caird*, the little fleet of vessels steered slowly through the jumble of ice. Before long they came to open water, free of ice, which they had not seen for well over a year.

But once in open seas there was no shelter from the brutal winds that tore down on the boats, sending huge waves crashing over the sides and tossing the vessels around like corks. Men bailed for their lives while others rowed.

Nor was there a friendly iceberg where they could pitch a tent or set up the stove to cook a hot meal. It meant the men had to eat raw dog food for lunch while bobbing about in rough seas. Many were sick.

Shackleton knew his men were getting weak. As darkness fell he took the huge risk of turning the vessels back into the shelter of the pack ice. Once protected against the worst winds, he hoped the men would be able to grab some much-needed sleep. It had been two days since they last slept properly.

The Boss was a giant to the weak, freezing men. During the day he always seemed to be standing upright at the tiller of the *Caird* as a symbol of defiance against the raging seas. At night he hardly slept and kept a constant watch over his men like a mother hen caring for her chicks.

Morning broke to find the seas whipped up by a roaring wind and the boats surrounded by large chunks of ice. It was impossible to sail. The only comfort was a drink of steaming hot milk.

When the winds eased, Shackleton set forth again. But the choppy seas and strong winds made it very hard going.

The biggest problem was the *Stancomb Wills,* the smallest boat. The *Wills* was less than 7m (20ft) long with a small sail and often fell behind the larger *James Caird* and *Dudley Docker* in the rough seas.

Shackleton was worried that the *Wills* would fall behind the *Caird* and the *Docker* and never be seen again. He kept a constant watch on the craft. Sometimes he fixed a rope between the *Caird* or the *Docker* and the *Wills* to tow the little boat along. Shackleton was determined to save his men – all of them.

Eight men were crammed into the *Wills*, which was under the command of Tom Crean. But two of Tom's men were very sick and unable to help sail the boat. Others were on the brink of collapse. All were cold, wet and hungry.

Once, the boat almost sank when a hefty wave swept over the vessel. Water poured in and the *Wills* looked doomed. But the next wave slammed into the boat, tipping it over and sending the floods of water back into the sea.

Slowly, the three vessels went back into the open seas. It was hard going. Pulling on the oars drained the men. Dinner was little more than cold dog food and biscuits and nothing could overcome their thirst. All the men were desperately thirsty. They had not taken enough drinking water on the journey. Sometimes they would break off a chunk of floating ice or they chewed slices of raw seal meat and sucked the blood for its moisture.

Even though they were very tired from rowing, the men found it hard to sleep. The temperature plunged below freezing. They shivered so much that they kept each other awake. The men clung to each other for warmth. They awoke in the morning looking like snowmen from the thick white covering of frost which had built up during the night.

The misery was made worse by a new danger – killer whales. When the men awoke they saw a pack of killer whales, each weighing around 8,000kg (8 tons), circling the boats. A man would only survive for seconds if he fell into the sea.

Shackleton quickly guided the boats away from the danger and hoped for calmer seas. It did not happen. Instead, boats rocked from side to side in the rolling and tumbling water. Almost all the crew were seasick.

To save weight Shackleton decided to dump some stores overboard. Before ditching some cases, the men ate as much food as they could, but it had to be eaten cold.

The extra food was not enough to help them. The cold and exhaustion were so bad that Shackleton knew a number of men were near the end. Some would not survive much longer unless the fleet of boats reached land as quickly as possible.

It was their sixth day at sea. Once again the boats were battered by a heavy swell and strong winds. At night, the three vessels came together for protection against the rough seas.

The night was bitterly cold. Sea spray froze as soon as it splashed over the vessels. Soon all the men were white with frost. Some could not stop shivering. One man slipped as he stood up and tumbled headlong into the sea. A quick-thinking sailor grabbed him and saved his life.

Shackleton tied a rope to the *Wills* because he feared it might be lost during the dark night. A storm soon blew up and the rope was stretched to breaking point. But the line held and the *Wills* was saved.

On the *Docker*, Skipper Worsley had not slept for days. He was exhausted and tried to grab some rest. He quickly fell into a very deep sleep. The other seamen grew alarmed when he did not wake up after a few hours.

They shouted and prodded Skipper but he did not move. In desperation one of the sailors kicked him. He still did not stir. He kicked him again. He did not move. They feared Skipper was dead. Finally one sailor gave Skipper a terrific kick. He groaned and opened his eyes, wanting to know what the fuss was all about.

Dawn broke on the seventh day at sea to bring a glorious sight – the mountain peaks of Elephant Island were visible on the distant horizon. The mountains were about 50km (30 miles) away and it was the first time in a week the men could smile.

Shackleton called for one last push to reach the island. But the men were on the point of collapse. Some had lost heart.

Even Shackleton felt the terrible strain. He had not slept properly for three nights. His face was frostbitten, he was wet through, very hungry and desperately thirsty. But the Boss did not let the strain show – he was determined to show his men he would not give in and they would all survive.

The weakest men were lumped together in Tom Crean's boat, the little *Wills*. Percy Blackborrow, the man who had secretly stowed away on *Endurance*, was in the worst condition. His feet had been soaked by freezing water for many days and were badly frostbitten. Now he had no feeling in his feet. Blackborrow, the youngest man on the expedition, was worried he would never walk again.

Shackleton saw that Blackborrow was very sick and tried to cheer him up. When the *Caird* pulled alongside the *Wills* that morning, he shouted: 'Blackborrow?' 'Here, sir,' Blackborrow called out in a weak voice. 'We shall be on Elephant Island soon,' Shackleton yelled back. 'No one has ever landed there before and you will be first ashore.'

All day the men pulled slowly towards the island. In the grim circumstances, the dark brooding mountain and fearsome glaciers looked liked paradise.

The light was fading and darkness drew near as the three boats came close to the island. Shackleton knew that another night at sea might be fatal for some men. He wanted to make a landing as quickly as possible.

But it was too late and too dark to risk a landing. To try to reach the shore in the dark they would risk hitting rocks and sinking. The only choice was to spend another terrible night at sea.

It was a miserable night. Temperatures plunged, winds roared and the sea spray froze as it splashed over the men crowded together. In the raging storm, the *Dudley Docker* became separated from the *Caird* and the *Wills*. Shackleton feared the boat had sunk.

The first rays of daylight brought little relief from the battering. The winds screeched and the men shivered from the piercing cold. Sadly, there was no sign of the *Dudley Docker*.

The one good thing was that the men were now able to get a quick drink. Lumps of ice, which had broken away from the big glaciers on Elephant Island, floated in the sea. Chunks were broken off and sucked – the first drink of water in days.

Shackleton stood up in the *James Caird* and gazed at Elephant Island. He could see a small beach. It was full of rocks and stones. Above it, a steep cliff towered upwards. An awful place. But there was no choice. He decided to go for it.

The *Caird* and the *Wills* were brought closer to the shore. But hopes of landing were dashed by the sight of ugly black rocks which poked out of the sea and blocked the path to shore.

At that moment the *Dudley Docker* suddenly came into view. The boat had survived a terrible night in the wild seas. Shackleton was overjoyed. All three vessels were together again.

Shackleton raced to get the men ashore before any new hazard hit them. He was anxious not to risk the *James Caird* getting wrecked on the rocks. So he clambered on board the *Stancomb Wills* with Tom Crean and steered towards shore.

The *Wills* sailed slowly up and down, searching for a gap. Soon a narrow channel was spotted in the jagged rocks. Shackleton lined up the boat at the ready and waited for a wave to roll towards the shore. The next wave came from behind the boat and carried the *Wills* through the gap onto the pebbly shore.

Chapter 12

TEARS AND FEARS

Shackleton jumped out of the boat. It was 497 days – almost one year and five months – since Shackleton had last stood on dry land.

Some men laughed out loud. Others cried. A few picked up stones from the beach and ran them through their fingers. Most could not believe it.

The firm ground beneath their feet felt strange. Some of the men found their legs were like rubber after so long at sea. But many were too weak to care. Frostbite, hunger and thirst had taken a heavy toll.

Shackleton tried to keep his promise that the injured Blackborrow should have the honour of being first ashore. But Blackborrow's feet were so sore he could not walk. He had to be carried up the beach.

Shackleton ordered a hot drink to be made from powdered milk. It warmed the men and lifted spirits. For a moment, their fate did not seem too bad.

That happy state did not last long. Shackleton soon realised the small beach was a death trap. He noticed marks from the tide on the cliff face. This was a sign that the beach was likely to be swamped by incoming tides. So next day the three little boats sailed down the coast and found a new, safer beach to build their camp.

Shackleton had named the beach Cape Wild after his friend, Frank Wild. But after a day or two of powerful winds the men changed the name to Cape Bloody Wild!

Shackleton knew Elephant Island was no place to be marooned though. No one lived there and no ships ever passed by.

Elephant Island is a tiny desolate place with narrow, pebbly beaches and steep cliffs leading to large mountains and dangerous glaciers. The weather is dreadful and the island was only discovered when a ship was blown off course in a storm.

The castaways were cut off from the rest of the world. They might as well have been stranded on a distant planet.

Freezing temperatures and winds, screeching to hurricane force, made life hell. Stones and chunks of ice were picked up and hurled along the beach by the 80 mph winds. One day, soon after landing on the beach, the wind roared to 120 mph.

Men were blown off their feet. A tent was ripped apart by the wind. Once the *Dudley Docker*, which had been taken out of the water for safety, was blown around the beach by the wind.

Shackleton faced a terrible choice – wait on the island and hope a ship might pass by or try to reach the nearest inhabited island.

But Shackleton knew that many of the castaways were too sick to take another long boat journey. Many had collapsed, while others were very weak. Shackleton had only one choice – to take a small party with him in search of rescue.

Shackleton's plan was to take the largest boat – the *James Caird* – and sail to the nearest place where a rescue ship could be found. It meant taking six men in the *Caird* and leaving 22 behind on Elephant Island to await rescue.

The best chance, he decided, was to sail across the mighty Southern Ocean to South Georgia – the island where the *Endurance* expedition had begun so long ago.

The fate of the 22 men depended entirely on Shackleton getting the *Caird* through to South Georgia. If the *Caird* sank, the castaways would also perish because no one knew they were stranded on the island. But Shackleton's men trusted the Boss and knew he would come back for them.

Work began immediately to make the *James Caird* ready for the long voyage. Planks were yanked off the *Dudley Docker* and *Stancomb Wills* to make the sides of the *Caird* a little higher, to stop too much water pouring in. The mast from the *Wills* was cut down and jammed into the hull to give added strength. Over 1,000kg (1 ton) of rocks were placed in the hull as ballast to make the *Caird* more stable in the rough seas.

A sail was rigged up from some spare canvas and decking was made from old food cases. The men plugged the gaps between the planks with an odd mixture of artist's oil paint, spare flour and seal's blood.

Shackleton's hardest decision was to choose men to sail on the

James Caird to South Georgia with him and those who would be forced to remain behind on the beach. It was a toss-up which faced the tougher ordeal.

Crossing the fearsome Southern Ocean in a small open boat was madness. It had never been attempted before. The Southern Ocean is the roughest on earth. Only desperate men would attempt such a voyage.

But the men left behind on Elephant Island faced terrible weeks or months of lonely isolation, violent storms and starvation. Nor could they be certain that Shackleton would get the *Caird* to South Georgia and bring a rescue ship.

Shackleton selected the tough Irishman Tom Crean and Skipper Frank Worsley, the captain of *Endurance*, who was also a very skilled navigator. The other three were carpenter Chippy McNish, seaman John Vincent and another Irish sailor called Tim McCarthy.

Shackleton asked his reliable old friend Frank Wild to remain behind in charge on Elephant Island.

Four weeks' of food supplies and two kegs of fresh water were loaded onto the *James Caird*. The six men took their places. South Georgia was almost 1,300km (800 miles) away across the worst seas on the planet.

On the beach, the 22 remaining men stood together watching the *Caird* pull away from the beach. They were a forlorn sight, cold and lashed by the winds. They knew Shackleton would need great luck to reach South Georgia.

But the castaways waved and raised a cheer as the *Caird* began the long journey. 'Good luck,' they yelled, although their words were drowned out by the roaring wind and crashing waves.

On board the *Caird*, Shackleton and his crew waved back. Often the little boat was lost behind the dark waves for a time and then reappeared. The men strained their eyes for a last glimpse. Then the *James Caird* disappeared from sight.

The Boss sailed with a promise to come back and rescue his men. That night one of the men left on the beach at Elephant Island jotted down a few words in his diary. He wrote: 'The *Caird* is our only hope.'

Chapter 13

THE GREATEST JOURNEY EVER

The tiny *James Caird* was like a toy in the vast, rowdy Southern Ocean. Giant waves seemed to dwarf the little craft and threatened to swallow it at any moment. The boat was tossed and thrown about. The chances of battling through to South Georgia looked very slim.

Ahead lay almost 1,300km (800 miles) of cruel seas, with huge waves 15m (50ft) high and powerful currents. Soon after leaving Elephant Island behind, the wind raced to over 30 mph and the boat was rocked from side to side in the rough rolling seas. Most on board were seasick.

For two days the little *Caird* travelled north, trying to escape from the last traces of ice surrounding Elephant Island. Then it set a new course to South Georgia.

From the start the omens were not good. Soon after sailing, Shackleton spotted something floating in the sea nearby. It was pieces of wreckage from a ship that had been sunk by the brutal seas.

The *James Caird* battled on. On board, the men tried hard to make themselves comfortable and stay as dry as possible.

But the six sailors were not equipped for a long boat voyage. They did not have waterproof or oilskin coats to protect them from the freezing water pouring into the boat. Their fur boots were useless against the constant waves and spray. Often they stood up to their knees in freezing water. All the men had frostbite and their trousers or woolly jumpers were never dry.

Shackleton knew that to withstand the constant battering the men would require regular hot meals. Twice a day hot mugs of hoosh were prepared and, in between, they enjoyed boiling hot drinks made from powdered milk.

Cooking was a major ordeal in the tumbling and rolling seas. Tom Crean was often the cook, hunched over the little stove because there was not enough room to sit upright. But it needed two others to support him and make sure the precious contents in the pot did not spill over as the *Caird* lurched about.

One man stayed at the tiller to steer the boat. Five other pairs of eyes were glued to the boiling pot of hoosh. Sometimes stray hairs from the reindeer sleeping bags fell into the pot and Tom would fish them out. To ensure that none of the hoosh was lost, he squeezed the hair dry over the boiling pot.

When it was ready the steaming hot food was gulped down. The first man to finish then leapt up to replace the man at the tiller.

Taking rest was difficult. The sleeping bags were placed on piles of stones and jammed between boxes of food. No one ever got a good night's sleep.

The cold carried a big risk for the *James Caird*. One morning the men awoke to discover the *Caird* was sitting very low in the water.

It was much lower than usual. To their horror, they found that the vessel was caked in ice which had built up during the night. The extra weight threatened to sink them.

The ice was about 30cms (1ft) thick and each splash of sea spray added a fresh layer to the icy coating. The boat's oars were frozen to the side of the vessel. If the seas became rougher the *Caird* would sink.

Shackleton quickly ordered each man to start chipping the ice off the sides and canvas covering of the *Caird*. It was a perilous task.

The men took it in turns to crawl along the deck with an axe to knock off the ice. Clinging on with one hand, the men chipped away with the other. It was a great strain in the rolling seas and no one could stay out on the decking for more than four or five minutes. Had a man lost his grip and fallen overboard there was no chance of rescue. But slowly, the men won the fight.

One night Shackleton was at the tiller, steering the *Caird* through the choppy seas. It was very dark and black clouds had shut out the moonlight.

Around midnight, Shackleton looked up and saw a white cloud appear on the horizon. He was puzzled because the sun was not due to rise for many hours. Shackleton called Skipper, Tom and the others to have a look at the odd cloud. 'It's clearing up, boys,' he said cheerfully.

Then he realised that the white line of cloud was moving. The 'cloud' was the crest of a giant wave. And the enormous wall of water was heading straight for the *Caird.*

'For God's sake, hold on!' Shackleton yelled. 'It's got us.'

The mighty wave slammed into the *Caird* and lifted the boat bodily out of the water. Everyone held their breath as the vessel was thrust forward like a cork and then crashed back into the sea. The six men were thrown around like dolls and water poured over the sides.

The rolling and tumbling stopped, almost as soon as it had begun, and the boat was still upright in the water. The *James Caird* had survived.

The six men were badly shaken. But they had no time to think. They were knee-deep in cold water and the boat was sinking fast. Grabbing every pot and mug they could lay their hands on, the men bailed frantically and flung the water over the sides. It took an hour to empty the boat. But the *James Caird* had survived another close encounter with death.

Shackleton knew the intense cold and strain of the voyage was affecting the men. They were all weak. Some were terrified.

Shackleton's gift for understanding his men was vital at this stage. He always put the safety and care of his men above everything else. He also knew how to lift spirits when things looked black.

If he saw someone struggling, Shackleton would have a few encouraging words with the man. Or he would order 'hot drinks' or a mug of warming hoosh for all hands.

For ten days the *Caird* fought the seas and terrible conditions. The deadly ocean fought back, sending hefty waves crashing over the sides.

Locating the small island of South Georgia was critical. The island lies in the vast, open expanse of water between the continents of South America and South Africa. There is no other land nearby.

Skipper Worsley was a key member of the party. He was a fine navigator whose skills were essential in finding South Georgia. Any error in the course he set for the *James Caird* would be disastrous.

After thirteen days of sailing he calculated that the *Caird* was less than 200km (125 miles) from South Georgia. That same day, a bird flew alongside the *Caird* – a clear sign that land was not far away.

But just when things began to look brighter a new hazard arose – thirst. The *James Caird* carried two barrels of fresh water which was collected from glaciers on Elephant Island. When the first was drained, the second barrel was opened.

But Shackleton discovered that the water was foul. Sea water, which is salty and cannot be drunk, had entered the barrel. To make matters worse, reindeer hairs from the sleeping bags had also found their way into the barrel.

First they tried filtering the water through a cloth. It took most of the revolting hairs away. But drinking the water fouled by the salty sea water only made them feel more thirsty. Their lips began to crack and their tongues, desperate for a drink, began to swell. It became hard to swallow food.

Spirits were raised next day when a few more birds began to flock around the boat in search of scraps. Shackleton also knew that this type of bird never flew more than 20km (12 miles) from dry land.

But no land could be seen. Skipper was worried. He might have made a mistake and an error in his reckoning would be fatal.

Suddenly the clouds parted and the black, snow-capped mountains of South Georgia appeared through the gap. 'Land!' someone shouted. The clouds quickly closed together again like someone drawing curtains and the mountains were gone from sight.

But nothing could take away their joy at finding the island. Skipper's navigation had been perfect. After fourteen days crossing the frightening Southern Ocean in an open boat, they had reached South Georgia. 'We've done it,' Shackleton whispered to himself.

The big task now was to find a place to land and to get some fresh water.

Darkness was falling and Shackleton knew it was dangerous to risk trying to land at night. Unseen rocks and reefs might sink the *Caird* just when they thought they were safe. Shackleton decided to keep the boat offshore during the night.

But soon after dark the Southern Ocean took full revenge on the *James Caird*. A mighty storm erupted and the vessel was flung around the sea. Water poured onto the deck. At times it seemed as though the *Caird* was full of water. In pitch darkness, the men once again grabbed anything that held water and bailed for their lives.

Shackleton said it was the worst storm he had ever seen in all his years at sea. Not far away, during the same storm, a 500-ton (510 kg) cargo ship sank with the loss of all the sailors on board.

The men battled with the storm throughout the night.

The wind, which grew to hurricane force by first daylight, roared to 80 mph during the day. It was impossible to hear what anyone said. But it was also impossible to try landing a boat in such a storm. The *Caird* would be smashed on the rocks.

Tired, cold and desperately thirsty, the men bailed and pumped out the water. Cooking was impossible in the raging turmoil. All day the fierce wind screamed down on the boat and the freezing spray lashed the men.

Landing in the storm was not possible. So the weary men faced another night at sea.

Shackleton wondered whether all six would survive another night afloat in the raging seas. Some were very near the end. 'The chance of surviving the night seemed small,' he said. 'I think most of us felt that the end was very near.'

It was a truly terrible night for the men in the *Caird*. Although the storm began to ease, the men were crying out for water. It had been two days since they last had a proper drink. By dawn, the only aim was to get fresh water.

Skipper wanted to sail around the island to the whaling stations where they would find men and ships. That was at least 150km

(95 miles) away, which meant another full day at sea. Shackleton rejected the idea. Two of the men were very weak and all six were in urgent need of water. Another day at sea would be too much.

The safety of his men came first. He insisted they land on South Georgia as fast as possible.

Shackleton steered the *Caird* along the rocky coast of South Georgia for several hours, each man straining his eyes for a suitable spot to land. By late afternoon they had still not found a safe place. Darkness was not far away. Another terrible night at sea without fresh drinking water threatened.

Skipper suddenly noticed a little cove that looked inviting. The *Caird* was steered towards the shore. But the approach was blocked by black rocks jutting out of the sea – like blackened teeth snarling at a visitor.

A closer inspection showed there was a narrow passage between the jagged rocks. It was just big enough for a boat. The men grabbed the oars and began rowing towards shore.

Shackleton stood up at the front, guiding the little craft through the dangerous rocks. He edged the boat into position at the opening of the gap and waited for a large wave. With a shove from behind, the wave hit the *Caird* and carried the boat onto the shore, where it came to a grinding stop on the wet stones.

Shackleton tumbled out of the *Caird* and hurt himself on the sharp rocks. But he managed to wrap the boat's rope around a boulder and the *Caird* was held fast. It was one year and five months since Shackleton had last set foot on South Georgia.

As the men clambered ashore they quickly noticed a stream of water trickling down the cliff face. Within seconds, the men fell to their knees and were gulping fresh water. No drink in the world ever tasted better.

The amazing voyage of the *James Caird*, which had lasted seventeen days, and is perhaps the greatest boat journey ever undertaken, was finally over.

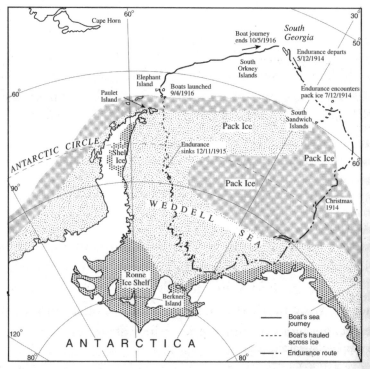

Endurance: the drift of the Endurance *through the Weddell Sea and the expedition's subsequent journeys to Elephant Island and South Georgia.*

Chapter 14

A TOUGH CHOICE

The rocky and bleak cove in South Georgia was like paradise to the exhausted men. A small cave was found which gave a little shelter against the fierce weather.

The stove was quickly lit and was soon pumping out mugfulls of steaming hot hoosh and warming drinks of milk. Then the men climbed into their sleeping bags for a well-earned rest.

But the Boss stayed up for hours, keeping a close eye on the *James Caird* and watching over his men. After a while he too grew tired and Tom Crean took over the watch.

The men were woken in the middle of the night to hear Tom shouting for help. Only half awake, they scrambled from their sleeping bags and found Tom splashing about up to his neck in the foaming seas clutching the *Caird*'s rope.

The wind had whipped up during the night and loosened the rope tying the *Caird* to the rocks. As the boat began to drift out to sea, Tom bravely plunged into the water and grabbed the rope.

Shackleton leapt into the water to help Tom and the *Caird* was saved. But no one slept very well for the rest of the night as they feared the *Caird* might break free again. In the morning the little boat was dragged up the beach away from the incoming waves.

The six men could not stay for long in the little cove, however. After a rest of five days, Shackleton ordered the men back into the *Caird* for a short trip of a few kilometres to a safer spot across the bay.

The new cove was a better place to make camp. Ample water flowed from nearby glaciers and Shackleton found seals and birds to provide the men with plenty of fresh meat.

But Shackleton's journey was not over.

The problem was that the *Caird* had landed on the south side of the island. The whaling stations, where there were men and ships, stood on the northern side. No one lived in the southern part. Shackleton and his men had to reach the north of the island quickly to find rescuers for those trapped on the beach at Elephant Island.

The easiest way was to sail the *James Caird* from the south to the north of the island. However, the *Caird* had been crippled by the boat journey from Elephant Island. The rudder, which is essential to steer a boat, had broken off during the landing on South Georgia. The *Caird* was not able to go to sea again.

Shackleton was left with no choice but to walk across the mountains and glaciers to reach the whaling stations on the north side of the island. It was another desperate gamble.

In a straight line, the cross-country journey was not very far, perhaps only 50km (32 miles). But no one had ever walked across South Georgia before. There were no maps to guide the travellers. Ahead lay miles of rocky mountains and huge glaciers

dotted with dangerous crevasses.

Not all the men from the *Caird* could make the cross-country march. Two of the sailors had collapsed from the strain of the boat journey and Shackleton needed one other to remain behind to nurse them.

This left only three men fit enough to walk across South Georgia's mountains and glaciers – the powerful Tom Crean, the great navigator Skipper Worsley and the Boss.

Shackleton decided to travel light. Carrying extra weight would slow them down. He wanted to make the trip as fast as possible. He abandoned his tent and sleeping bags. Shackleton, Tom and Skipper were poised to tackle the freezing mountains without any shelter.

All they carried was a small cooking stove and a hoosh pot. Each man took three days' food, wrapped in a spare sock. A 15m (50ft) length of rope was taken, a box of matches and a carpenter's tool called an adze, which was used as an ice-axe.

Lumps of cloth were cut up to make an extra pocket in each man's coat. Inside the pocket, each man carried personal gear, such as a spoon for the hoosh, a few biscuits and some tobacco.

The reindeer-skin boots worn by the men were a big problem. The flat smooth soles of the boots would be lethal on the glassy ice. To provide some grip, screws were pulled from the sides of the *James Caird* and hammered through the soles of their boots.

Shackleton was ready for the march. A last hot meal was cooked. At 2 o'clock in the morning, Tom, Skipper and the Boss shook hands with the three men being left behind.

Slowly Shackleton, Tom and Skipper began the historic crossing of South Georgia. As the first steps were taken, the moon popped out from behind the dark clouds and gave the three men a welcome splash of light to help guide them over the mountains and glaciers. It was a good omen.

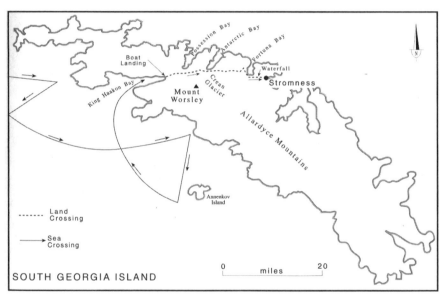

South Georgia was largely unexplored when Shackleton, Worsley and Tom Crean marched across the mountainous, glacier-strewn island in 1916. The map shows the path taken by the James Caird *approaching the island and the route across the island.*

Chapter 15

CROSSING SOUTH GEORGIA

A line of dark mountains stood in the path of Shackleton, Tom and Skipper as the march began. Their goal – the whaling stations – lay on the other side of the mountains. In the eerie moonlight the barrier looked very frightening.

For two hours the men climbed up an icy slope, reaching a height of 750m (2,500ft). Sometimes they slipped and fell in the dark. The make-do crampons on their boots did little to stop them slipping. Luckily no one fell into a crevasse.

As dawn broke a thick blanket made it impossible to see very far ahead. And they could hardly even see each other.

In the haze the men came dangerously close to disaster. Unable to see far ahead, the three men stumbled close to the edge of a vast crevasse. A few more steps and they would have crashed to their deaths. Shackleton grabbed the rope and all three were quickly tied together for safety.

Shackleton led the group, striding ahead in the misty gloom. From behind, Tom and Skipper yelled directions as though the men were still at sea – 'port' (left), 'starboard' (right) or 'steady' (straight ahead).

A little later the fog began to lift. Suddenly the men could see the land ahead. What they saw lifted their spirits – a frozen lake.

The lake was good news. Travelling across a flat frozen lake would be easier than scrambling up glaciers or climbing mountains.

But it was not a lake. The men soon realised it was a vast bay and they had come in the wrong direction. Cursing their luck, Shackleton, Tom and Skipper turned around and headed back to the icy slopes.

Once on the slope the men came face to face with the chain of five mountain peaks which blocked their way to the whaling stations. The mountains were like the knuckles of a clenched fist. The best move was to find a pass between the mountains.

Shackleton took what seemed to be the easiest route.

A grim sight awaited the men at the top of the slope. Looking down the other side, they saw a steep cliff of ice. It was impossible to climb down. For the second time that day, Shackleton, Tom and Skipper had to turn around and retrace their steps.

Shackleton wanted to cheer Tom and Skipper so he ordered a hot mug of hoosh. The heat of the food gave their bodies new strength and the men looked for another pass through the mountains.

After choosing a new route, the three were quickly on the march again. Up they climbed, often sinking to their thighs in soft snow. It was very tiring. After only twenty minutes of climbing the men collapsed in the snow, gasping for breath.

A fresh blow awaited the men at the top of the slope. The land ahead was even worse than at the top of the first slope. Yet it was too dangerous to consider trying to climb down.

Skipper was very tired and wanted to hazard the climb down the steep icy slope. But Shackleton refused to risk the lives of his men. Once again they had to turn around and go back the way they came.

It was a bitter blow. Even worse, the men could not afford to waste time. Without the shelter of a tent or sleeping bag, they ran the risk of getting caught in the open when night-time temperatures plunged.

Shackleton was horrified when he realised that night was approaching fast. Even worse, a new blanket of fog was falling in the area. The men were stuck about 1,500m (4,500ft) up the icy slope without shelter. They would freeze to death if they stayed on the slope, where temperatures are lower than on the ground.

Shackleton quickly ordered the men to get down the icy slope as fast as possible. It was hard going and they risked a fall. The sun began to disappear behind the mountains and darkness began to fall. Shackleton knew the men were in great peril.

The situation was desperate and it called for desperate measures. 'We've got to take a risk,' Shackleton stated. He looked around for a quick way down the slope. They would slide down the mountain, he announced.

The 15m (50ft) of rope was coiled into three circles like three mats.

Shackleton sat in front, with Skipper in the middle and Tom at the back. Skipper locked his arms and legs around Shackleton and Tom did the same to Skipper. They were locked together, like a toboggan.

With a mighty yell, Shackleton kicked off and the three men hurtled down the hill. The wind whistled past their ears as the toboggan picked up speed. Shackleton, Tom and Skipper screamed aloud in a mixture of excitement and sheer terror.

In the darkness, it was impossible to see the bottom of the slope. Crashing into a rock on the way down would spell certain disaster. The toboggan was racing into the unknown and no one knew where it would stop. The land around them was a blur as they shot into space.

Suddenly the toboggan ran into soft snow and began to slow down. In an instant the three men came to a crashing halt against a bank of deep, soft snow.

The men tumbled over and over. Slightly dazed, they rose to their feet. All three had survived the nightmare descent. The only mishap was that Skipper's trousers had been ripped.

But there was no time to celebrate. A mug of warming hoosh was quickly brewed and the march started again soon after. The moon appeared from behind the clouds and gave a little light to help guide the way ahead.

By midnight Shackleton, Tom and Skipper had been walking for

21 hours. Slowly the men plodded onwards. Soon they came upon a new icy slope which led towards a bay. But it was not the bay where the whaling stations stood.

Once again, the three men had to turn round and go back the way they came. It was another bitter disappointment. But they had no choice – it was march or die.

At around 5 o'clock in the morning the three stopped for a break. It was freezing cold and the men were desperate for sleep. Dawn was approaching and they had been on the march for 26 hours. Lying close together for warmth, Tom and Skipper began to doze off to sleep.

Shackleton knew that falling asleep in freezing temperatures was fatal – they would freeze to death. After just five minutes, Shackleton woke Tom and Skipper and told them they had been asleep for half an hour.

The men were quickly back on their feet and walking once again. At the top of a slope a wonderful sight greeted them. The sun had risen and in the morning light the three men could pick out a bay – the bay where the whaling fleets were stationed. Their goal was in sight.

Shackleton ordered a hot mug of hoosh before they set out for the final leg of their journey. It was their last hot food. The cooking pot was thrown away.

Suddenly Shackleton called for quiet. He thought he heard a sound. It sounded faintly like a whistle. Or maybe his mind was playing tricks.

Shackleton knew the whaling stations called the men to work by blowing a whistle and that the men at the whaling station started work at 7 o'clock in the morning.

Shackleton, Tom and Skipper grabbed a watch and looked at the time. The hands were ticking slowly towards 7 o'clock. The three men stood in silence watching the hands move slowly towards seven. The only sound to be heard was the faint tick of the watch. The tension was agonising.

Bang on time, at 7 o'clock, the whistle rang out. The men broke into broad grins and shook hands. It was the first sound from the outside world they had heard for nearly eighteen months.

Overjoyed at their luck, the trio pressed on. There were, however, still glaciers and ice-fields to cross. Their food was almost gone and they had not slept for nearly a day and a half. And danger was always near.

Once, Tom crashed through weak ice and fell into freezing water. He was pulled out but he did not have any spare clothes, so he marched on with soaking wet feet and trousers.

By early afternoon the three men stood at the top of a hill, gazing down on the whaling station at the port of Stromness, which was spread out below them. It was a drop of around 750m (2,500ft). Below they could pick out ships, buildings and the tiny figures of men hurrying about their work.

The men began to climb down. At first they made good progress. Then they came to a stream and followed it for a short while before the stream came to a sudden halt at the edge of a ridge. The water then plunged over the edge in a waterfall.

Shackleton was so tired he could hardly think straight. But he knew that turning back was out of the question. It was late afternoon and darkness was not many hours away. They were shivering with cold and all their food had gone. Another night in the open was out of the question.

Shackleton acted fast. He grabbed the rope and tied it fast to a rock. 'We'll climb down, boys,' he said.

The waterfall was about 10m (30ft) long. Tom, the largest of the three men, went down first. The stream of icy, cold water drenched him. Next Shackleton had to endure the cold shower from the waterfall and Skipper was last down.

At the bottom the three drenched men had no time to dry off or hang up their soaking wet clothes. The Stromness whaling station was not far away. But the sun was setting and temperatures dropped sharply after dark.

The three men walked as fast as their tired legs would allow. They were near to collapse. But the end of the remarkable journey was finally in sight. For once, they could afford a faint smile.

Shackleton had left South Georgia for the Antarctic only eighteen months earlier. The party had set out with 28 well-fed, fit men and a new expedition ship stocked with food and supplies for several years.

Now Shackleton, Tom and Skipper were a terrible sight. They had not washed or shaved for months. They smelt disgusting. Their hair was long and matted with grime and grease from the cooking stove. The three filthy, black faces were lined from exhaustion and frostbite. Their clothes were torn and ragged.

Tired, cold and hungry, the three men stumbled along. The final few kilometres seemed to take ages.

In the distance they saw two figures. Slowly the figures took shape. They were two boys, aged about ten or twelve who were playing near the harbour. The boys looked up in horror to see what looked like three scarecrows coming towards them, then fled in terror.

Soon after they saw an old man. As the three men walked slowly towards him, the terrified man turned and hurried away as the boys had done. Slowly, Shackleton, Tom and Skipper began to understand just how terrible they looked.

They shuffled slowly towards the harbour where they found a whaling foreman. Shackleton stepped forward and asked if they could be taken to the station manager's office.

The foreman took them to the office, but he insisted they stand outside. A few minutes later the station manager came outside. He was shocked at the dreadful state of the three men.

Shackleton recognised the station manager. They had met before *Endurance* sailed from South Georgia. But the manager

did not recognise the filthy wreck of a man who stood before him. Most people thought Shackleton and his crew were lost in the ice and dead.

'Who the hell are you?' the station manager asked.

Shackleton looked up and said: 'My name is Shackleton.'

The whaling foreman was so moved by their incredible story of survival that he turned away as tears welled up in his eyes.

Chapter 16

SAVED!

The hot water felt strange. Shackleton had not sat in a hot bath for almost two years.

Soon the three men shaved off their long beards, cut their hair and put on some clean clothes which the men at the whaling station had given them. Then they sat down to a massive dinner. That night they slept in a warm bed for the first time in many months.

Skipper borrowed one of the whaling ships to pick up the three men left behind with the *James Caird* on the other side of South Georgia. But his shipmates did not recognise Skipper when he landed in the bay – he was too clean!

Shackleton did not waste time at Stromness. He searched around for a ship that could make the voyage back to Elephant Island to rescue his 22 men. He found a ship called the *Southern Sky* which was suitable. But he could not find the owners to ask for their permission to take the ship. So he borrowed the vessel without permission.

Three days after Shackleton, Tom and Skipper staggered into the Stromness whaling station, the three men were on board the *Southern Sky* steaming towards Elephant Island. Unfortunately, the *Southern Sky* was not built to battle against the heavy pack ice in the Southern Ocean.

The *Southern Sky* sailed to within 100km (60 miles) of Elephant

Island. But the ice then blocked the ship's path. Even if they broke through the ice, there was a risk the ship would not be able to escape from Elephant Island. Shackleton could not risk this. The *Southern Sky* was turned round and steered back to port.

It was almost five weeks since Shackleton had left Elephant Island to reach South Georgia in the little *James Caird.*

Across the horizon, 100km (60 miles) away, the 22 men on the beach at Elephant Island had no idea that rescue had been so close. Each day they stood on the beach, hoping to catch sight of a ship. But none came.

Conditions on the island were terrible. The two lifeboats, *Dudley Docker* and *Stancomb Wills,* were turned upside down to provide shelter and the men were crammed together underneath like sardines in a can.

Food was scarce. At first they found enough penguins and seals to make hot meals. But when winter arrived the wildlife began to disappear and the men became more and more hungry. Sometimes they managed to scrape shellfish off the rocks to make weak soup.

The beach was little more than 100m (300ft) wide and winds battered the area. Often men were blown off their feet and rocks and lumps of ice were hurled around.

At first the men thought Shackleton would come back with a ship after only a month. Others feared the *James Caird* had sunk in the fierce Southern Ocean and they would never be rescued. As the weeks passed the men became more and more gloomy. Some thought they would never get off Elephant Island.

The mood was not helped by the awful condition of some men. The worst sufferer was Blackborrow, the stowaway. His frostbitten feet had turned rotten. Two months after landing on the island, the doctors had to operate to cut off some of his toes. Luckily, there were enough drugs to put Blackborrow to sleep for 55 minutes while the doctors operated.

Shackleton needed a bigger ship able to tackle the ice. In desperation, he went to South America where he asked the government of countries like Argentina, Chile and Uruguay to lend him a ship.

Uruguay came forward and offered a trawler. The trawler, which was named *Instituto de Pesca No 1*, sailed two days after Blackborrow's operation. Also on board were the faithful Tom and Skipper.

The ship made good progress. Shackleton was pleased that ice conditions were fairly good.

After only three days at sea, the mountains of Elephant Island could be spotted on the distant horizon. The ship pressed on and Shackleton was hopeful.

But the *Instituto de Pesca No 1* was soon stopped in its tracks by a line of thick ice. The tops of Elephant Island's mountains could clearly be seen. They were only 32km (20 miles) from the beach. However, it was not possible to break through the ice and the *Instituto de Pesca No 1* had to turn around and head back to port.

Weeks passed, and still the men on the beach at Elephant Island waited for rescue. Shackleton went back to Chile where he found a new ship, the *Emma*.

The small wooden ship was simply not strong enough to fight the rough seas and thick ice though. *Emma* met a belt of ice about 160km (100 miles) off the coast of Elephant Island. Further progress was not possible. With a heavy heart, Shackleton turned around and went back to South America.

It was the third defeat.

On Elephant Island the men knew nothing of Shackleton's three attempts at rescue. But they did know time was running out. Shackleton had been gone for almost four months. Supplies were low.

Each day the crisis on Elephant Island grew worse. Further weeks passed as Shackleton tried desperately to find another ship.

The government of Chile kindly lent Shackleton a new ship called the *Yelcho*. With Tom and Skipper again on board, Shackleton set off to make his fourth attempt at reaching the men stranded on the beach at Elephant Island.

Yelcho was not ideal for the task of navigating through the ice. But luck was on their side as the ship pressed on through the Southern Ocean. The weather was quite good and there was little sign of pack ice.

But hopes were dashed when a heavy fog fell on the area. It was impossible to see ahead and the sailors were worried that *Yelcho* might hit an iceberg in the murky gloom.

Shackleton had only one thing on his mind though – to rescue his men. Seizing control of the ship, he decided to push his luck and steer blindly into the fog. *Yelcho* was driven forward, regardless of the risk.

Luckily the fog began to lift as dawn broke. More importantly, daylight showed there was no ice in the area. *Yelcho* steamed on towards Elephant Island.

On the beach the men were doing their usual daily tasks. Some were preparing the miserable lunch whilst others cleaned up the mess around the upturned boats.

Two men were searching among the rocks for shellfish to make soup. One looked up and saw a dark shape on the horizon. He thought it was an iceberg. When he looked again he saw smoke coming from the distant shape.

Mayhem erupted. Men rushed out from under boats. The cooking pot was knocked over in the scramble. One man put his boots on the wrong feet and another tried to start a fire to signal the ship. Someone else carried the crippled Blackborrow outside to witness the wonderful scene.

Shackleton clambered down the rope and jumped into the *Yelcho's* lifeboat. Alongside him was Tom Crean. The boat was quickly rowed towards shore. The men on the beach waved frantically. Shackleton waved back. Some were in tears at being rescued at last.

Shackleton stood up in the boat and began counting the figures he could see running around the beach. First two, then four, then six, eight and ten. At last he cried out: 'They are all there. Every one of them. They are all saved.'

Shackleton was delighted. He had saved his men. 'Are you all well?' he shouted. 'We are all well, Boss,' came the reply.

But there was no time to celebrate. Shackleton did not want to hang around on Elephant Island. He was worried that the pack ice might close around the island and stop *Yelcho* from escaping.

Shackleton was in such a rush he did not even bother to visit the castaways' home under the two boats. Within an hour, all 22 men had been plucked from the beach and were safely on board the *Yelcho*, heading back to South America.

It had been four and a half months since Shackleton had sailed in the *James Caird* to bring a rescue ship. He had promised to come back and get his men. And he had overcome the mighty Southern Ocean and walked across the fearsome mountains and glaciers of South Georgia to do it.

Chapter 17

A LAST VOYAGE TO THE ICE

Shackleton never lost his love of adventure. Even the dramatic hardship of the *Endurance* voyage did not stop him dreaming of fresh expeditions.

By 1920, just four years after rescuing his men from Elephant Island, the Boss had a new expedition in mind.

The plan was to explore the Arctic Ocean. He had never ventured to the Arctic north. He even dreamed of getting to the North Pole.

Shackleton found it hard to raise money to pay for the expedition and his plans to explore the Arctic began to collapse. In desperation, he decided to go back to the area he knew best – the Antarctic.

A few rich friends came to his rescue and gave Shackleton the money for his voyage. He bought a ship called the *Quest* and announced he would sail around the entire Antarctic continent – a long voyage of almost 50,000km (30,000 miles).

He gathered a few old friends from his earlier expeditions to sail on the *Quest*. His men came from around the world to join the Boss on his new expedition.

On board with Shackleton was Frank Wild from the *Nimrod* and

Endurance expeditions. Skipper Worsley, who had navigated the *James Caird* on the incredible voyage to South Georgia, also went along. Other shipmates included the old sailor who hid the Bible under his jumper and the banjo player.

Quest was brought to London to make final preparations for the trip. The ship was moored alongside Tower Bridge on the River Thames. It was just a short distance from London Bridge, where as a young lad Shackleton first attempted to go to sea.

Shackleton said goodbye to his wife, Emily, and kissed his three children, Raymond, Cecily and Edward.

They never saw him again.

The *Quest* expedition, which was Shackleton's fourth voyage to the ice, sailed from London in September 1921. Crowds lined the docks and waved farewell.

Shackleton was happy again. He came alive at sea or on a tough trek across the ice. A job in an office or factory did not appeal to his nature. He wanted adventure, danger and the constant search for new horizons.

Quest drove south. All the men were looking forward to the expedition. What they did not notice was that Shackleton did not feel well.

The ship passed the tip of South America and headed towards South Georgia. All the well-known mountains and glaciers came into view. Shackleton felt at home.

Quest pulled into a little place called Grytviken. Shackleton knew it well. It was the spot where the whaling captains had warned him not to risk taking *Endurance* into the icy waters of the Weddell Sea only a few years earlier.

Shackleton went on deck and glanced at the snow-topped mountains and massive glaciers. It was a sight he knew well and loved very much. It was to be his last view of the ice and snow.

Shackleton went below to his cabin. He picked up his pen and began to write up his diary for the day, 4 January 1922. His last entry read: 'In the darkening twilight I saw a lone star hover, gem-like above the bay.'

In the early hours of 5 January 1922 Shackleton felt unwell. He called for the expedition's doctor. Shackleton poked a little fun at the doctor and asked: 'You're always wanting me to give up things. What is it I ought to give up?'

Minutes later Shackleton was dead.

Emily Shackleton asked that her husband be buried on South Georgia. Today Sir Ernest Shackleton, the Boss, one of the greatest explorers who ever lived, lies in the small cemetery overlooking the bay at Grytviken. His grave is surrounded by the glaciers, mountains, snow and ice he loved so well.

SIR ERNEST SHACKLETON – TIMELINE

1874 15 February   Born at Kilkea House, near Athy, County Kildare, Ireland,
son of Henry and Henrietta Shackleton

1884   Shackleton family moves to England

1890   Leaves school and joins merchant navy, aged sixteen
Makes first voyage in the sailing ship, *Houghton Tower*

1901   Joins Captain Scott's *Discovery* expedition to the Antarctic

1902 January   Sees the Antarctic Continent for the first time
2 November   Starts sledging journey with Scott and Wilson
30 December Reaches record 'furthest south'

1903 3 February   Arrives back at *Discovery*
1 March   Leaves Antarctica on the *Morning*

1904 9 April   Marries Emily Dorman in London

1905 2 February   Son, Raymond, born

1906 23 December   Daughter, Cecily, born

1907   Prepares *Nimrod* expedition to reach South Pole
30 July   *Nimrod* sails from London

1908 January   *Nimrod* arrives in the Antarctic
29 October   Starts march to the South Pole

1909 9 January   Reaches 'furthest south' – 179km (112 statue miles or 97
geographic miles) from South Pole – and abandons march
1 March   Arrives at *Nimrod*
14 June   Returns to London
14 December Receives knighthood

1911	15 July	Son, Edward, born
1913		Reveals plans to march across Antarctic Continent
1914	1 August	*Endurance* expedition leaves London
1915	19 January	*Endurance* trapped in the Weddell Sea
	27 October	*Endurance* abandoned and camp built on the ice
	21 November	*Endurance* sinks
1916	9 April	Lifeboats sail for Elephant Island
	15 April	Lands at Elephant Island
	24 April	Launches *James Caird* on boat journey to South Georgia
	10 May	Lands at South Georgia
	19 May	Starts trek across South Georgia
	20 May	Reaches Stromness whaling station
	23 May	Sails *Southern Sky* to rescue men on Elephant Island
	28 May	*Southern Sky* abandons rescue mission
	10 June	Sails *Instituto de Pesca No 1* in second rescue attempt
	13 June	*Instituto de Pesca No 1* abandons rescue mission near Elephant Island
	12 July	*Emma* launches third attempt to reach Elephant Island
	21 July	*Emma* abandons rescue attempt
	25 August	*Yelcho* launches fourth attempt to reach Elephant Island
	30 August	*Yelcho* reaches Elephant Island and rescues castaways
	3 September	Party returns to South America
1920		Plans new Polar expedition
1921	18 September	*Quest* expedition leaves London for the Antarctic
1922	4 January	Arrives at Grytviken, South Georgia
	5 January	Dies on board *Quest*, aged 47

FURTHER INFORMATION

Temperatures

In Shackleton's time, temperatures were measured in the Fahrenheit scale whereas today we mostly use Celsius. Rough comparisons are given but for those who wish to do their own conversions the calculations are:

To convert
Fahrenheit ° to Celsius °
   Subtract 32, divide by 1.8 (e.g. 68°F minus 32 divided by 1.8 = 20°C)

Celsius° to Fahrenheit°
   Multiply by 1.8, add 32 (e.g. 20°C x 1.8 = 36 + 32 = 68°F)

Temperature comparisons

°F	°C
98.4° (body temp)	36.9°
32 (water freezes)	0°
14	-10°
-4	-20°
-22	-30°
-40°	-40°

Distances

Distances in Shackleton's time were measured in feet (ft), yards (yds) and miles while today we use the metric system of centimetres (cms), metres (m) and kilometres (km). Weights were measured in ounces (oz), pounds (lbs) and tons compared with the modern day grams and kilograms (kgs).

To convert

Metres (m) to feet (ft)	multiply by 3.28
Feet (ft) to metres (m)	multiply by 0.30
Metres (m) to yards (yds)	multiply by 1.09
Yards (yds) to metres (m)	multiply by 0.91
Kilometres (km) to miles	multiply by 0.61
Miles to kilometres (km)	multiply by 1.61

Weights

To convert

Pounds (lbs) to kilograms (kgs)	multiply by 0.45
Kilograms (kgs) to pounds (lbs)	multiply by 2.20
Tons to kilograms (kgs)	multiply by 1016
Kilograms (kgs) to tons	multiply by 0.000984

FURTHER READING

Books

Alexander, Caroline   *Mrs Chippy's Last Expedition*, Bloomsbury

Hooper, Meredith   *A is for Antarctica*, Pan Books

Huntford, Roland   *Shackleton*, Hodder & Stoughton

Lonely Planet Guide   *Antarctica*, Lonely Planet

Shackleton, Jonathan &

John MacKenna   *Shackleton – An Irishman in Antarctica*, Lilliput Press

Smith, Michael   *An Unsung Hero – Tom Crean Antarctic Survivor*,
The Collins Press/Headline Publishing

Smith, Michael   *Iceman*, The Collins Press

Summers, Julie   *The Shackleton Voyages*, Weidenfeld & Nicolson

Videos

Shackleton: Escape From Antarctica, Crossing The Line Films, Co Wicklow, Ireland

South, Frank Hurley, National Film and Television Archive, 1919: BFI Video Publishing, London, UK

Websites

Antarctic Circle	www.Antarctic-circle.org
Antarctic Project	www.Asoc.org
British Antarctic Survey	www.Nerc-bas.ac.uk
Cool Antarctica	www.Coolantarctica.com
Heritage Antarctic	www.Heritage-Antarctica.org
James Caird Society	www.Jamescairdsociety.com
Scott Polar Research Institute	www.Spri.cam.ac.uk
70South	www.70South.com

INDEX